C000045610

The Adventures of
Sir Samuel White Baker

The Adventures of
Sir Samuel White Baker

Victorian Hero

M.J. TROW

First published in Great Britain in 2010 by
PEN & SWORD DISCOVERY
An imprint of
Pen & Sword Books Ltd
47 Church Street
Barnsley
South Yorkshire
S70 2AS

Copyright © M.J. Trow, 2010

ISBN 978-1-84884-178-9

The right of M.J. Trow to be identified as the author of this work has been asserted
by him in accordance with the Copyright, Designs and Patents Act 1988.

A CIP catalogue record for this book is
available from the British Library.

All rights reserved. No part of this book may be reproduced or transmitted in
any form or by any means, electronic or mechanical including photocopying,
recording or by any information storage and retrieval system, without
permission from the Publisher in writing.

Typeset by Concept, Huddersfield, West Yorkshire
Printed and bound in Great Britain by the MPG Books Group

Pen & Sword Books Ltd incorporates the imprints of Pen & Sword Aviation,
Pen & Sword Maritime, Pen & Sword Military, Wharncliffe Local History,
Pen & Sword Select, Pen & Sword Military Classics, Leo Cooper,
Remember When, Seaforth Publishing and Frontline Publishing.

For a complete list of Pen & Sword titles please contact
PEN & SWORD BOOKS LIMITED
47 Church Street, Barnsley, South Yorkshire, S70 2AS, England
E-mail: enquiries@pen-and-sword.co.uk
Website: www.pen-and-sword.co.uk

Contents

List of Plates   vii

1. The White Man's Burden   1
2. The Bakers' Half-Dozen   11
3. Newera Ellia   21
4. Eight Years' Wandering   33
5. Taking a Stroll   45
6. 'Flooey'   55
7. Into the Dark Continent   65
8. The Lake of Dead Locusts   81
9. 'Sacrifices to Geography'   95
10. Baker Pasha   107
11. Dancing with Baker   117
12. Val's Affair   129
13. The Traveller   141
14. The Journey Taken Alone   151
15. The Boy's Own Hero   161

Notes   167
Select Bibliography   173
Index   175

List of Plates

Samuel Baker on his return from the governor-generalship of the Sudan.

Florence Baker on her return from the Sudan.

A hippopotamus rams the Bakers' *diahbiah* on the Nile.

The engineers brought the steamers in sections across the desert.

Samuel Baker (in the foreground) leads his 'Forty Thieves'.

Wherever the Bakers went, they set the slaves free.

Baker's men hauling steamer No. 10 through the sudd.

Samuel Baker as the Apostle of Liberty from *Judy* magazine.

Baker of the Tenth.

Headquarters of the Royal Geographical Society in Savile Row.

Samuel Baker lectures to the Royal Geographical Society.

The last official photograph of Samuel Baker.

The governor general and his retinue.

Chapter 1

The White Man's Burden

'In commencing this subject,' wrote Samuel White Baker in his second book,[1] 'I must assume that the conquerors of territory are responsible for the moral welfare of the inhabitants; therefore our responsibility increases with our conquests. A mighty onus thus rests upon Great Britain, which few consider when they glory in the boast "that the sun never sets upon her dominions".' What Baker was describing (in 1854) would dominate almost every aspect of British life for the next century – the rise of new imperialism, its awesome responsibilities and fragilities and its final collapse, from which the country is still recovering.

Baker had seen, first-hand in Ceylon[2] in the 1840s and 1850s, the jungle-clad ruins of once great civilizations, and, unlike many of his desk-bound contemporaries in Whitehall, he realized that this would one day be the fate of the British civilization too:

> When the pomps and luxuries of Eastern cities spread throughout Ceylon and millions of inhabitants fed on her fertility, when the hands of her artists chiselled the figures of her gods from the rude rock, when her vessels, laden with ivory and spices, traded with the West, what were we? A forest-covered country, peopled by a fierce race of savages clad in skins, bowing before individual idolatry, paddling along our shores in frames of wickerwork and hide.[3]

Baker posed the question; what had happened? The East (by which he meant India and especially Ceylon) had declined and the West (by which he meant Britain) had risen. The forest was replaced by fertile fields, the coracles were now 'the taut spars of England's navy'. The hamlet had been superseded by the 'never-weary din of commerce' rolling through the 'city of the world'. Locomotives rattled along their rails, black-smoking steamers ploughed the oceans, 'the telegraph cripples time'.

In a couple of paragraphs Baker the gifted writer describes what happened next: 'It was then that the powers of the world were armed against her [Britain] and all Europe joined to tear the laurels from her crown ... the thunder of the cannon shook the world ... and war and tumult shrieked like a tempest over the fair face of Nature.' Baker asked himself whether the triumph of Britain, the creation in his own lifetime of the greatest empire the world had ever known, was by chance or was the 'mighty will of Omnipotence'.

Forty years later the 'poet of Empire', Rudyard Kipling, was attempting to answer the same question, and he traced the same progress in verse:

> Once, two hundred years ago, the trader came
>   Meek and tame.
> Where his timid foot first halted, there he stayed,
>   Till mere trade
> Grew to Empire and he sent his armies forth
>   South and North
> Till the country from Peshawar to Ceylon
>   Was his own.[4]

Having lost the thirteen colonies in North America, Britain began to expand elsewhere in the world. From three tiny 'factories' (trading posts) in Bombay, Madras and Bengal (all of which Samuel Baker was to visit on his travels), the East India Company spread its tentacles inland. Backed by its own armies and stiffened by government support, 'John Company' first removed the French rivalry of the Compagnie des Indes, then set about taking a subcontinent. From 1805 onwards, subsequent governors-general made treaties with native princes or put armies in the field against them. In the Carnatic, Tipu Sahib was defeated by Arthur Wellesley, the future Duke of Wellington. The fierce hill fighters the Gurkhas, who became a loyal element of the British army, were defeated by 1816. The Sindhis collapsed against General Napier in 1845 and the most formidable enemy the British faced in India, the Sikhs, were subjugated after two wars in the same decade. The British turned east into Burma in the 1820s and in India brought down Oudh and the remaining Maratha kingdoms.

The Sepoy War or Indian Mutiny which took place soon after Samuel Baker left Ceylon can hardly be regarded as the beginnings of Indian nationalism, but Anglo-Indian relations would never be the same again. The East India Company was broken up and the subcontinent run directly by Queen Victoria's government as the Raj; Whitehall, not Leadenhall Street,[5] now called the shots.

While Samuel Baker and his brothers John and Valentine were farming in Ceylon, their equivalents in India proper were building schools, railways and training up the most apt natives for menial work in the civil service of the future. By 1877, when Samuel Baker had been governor-general on another continent, Prime Minister Benjamin Disraeli had created Victoria Queen Empress, and the 'great white mother's' statues and portraits appeared in huge numbers all over India.

In Australia and New Zealand, similar exploitation of the native population occurred. After the loss of Georgia as a convict colony in British North America, New South Wales on the Australian mainland and Tasmania (Van Diemen's Land) fulfilled the same purpose. It was with difficulty that 'respectable' settlers made a new home for themselves among the sweepings of British gaols and the whalers plying their dangerous trade in Antarctic waters. Between 1780 and the end of Victoria's reign (1901) the 750,000 aboriginal natives had been reduced to 10 per cent of that figure, the rest having been wiped out by open skirmish warfare and a lack of resistance to Western disease. The discovery of gold in Australia in 1851 speeded up the process, although the drought of the central land mass precluded the sort of intense development that happened elsewhere.

In New Zealand the Maori were a more stubborn opponent, skilled after the 1820s in the use of firearms, and they put up an organized resistance in their *pa* (forts) in the Taramaki and Waikato wars in the 1860s. They lost, but managed to retain certain rights to their lands, still feeling bitter about the *te Riri pakeha*, the white man's anger, well into the twentieth century.

In Africa, which was to claim most of Samuel Baker's time and energy, the sheer size of the continent defied European control for nearly two centuries. In the north-east, south of Egypt in what became the Sudan, various tribes fought each other before the coming of the white man. Muslim since the eighth century, they declared *jihad* (holy war) against each other until well into the nineteenth century. In 1821 the Khedive (ruler) of Egypt, Mohammed Ali, conquered the Sudan and set up his capital at Khartoum on the Nile.

By 1830 the French had settled in Algeria in the far north-west and after bitter fighting made the area a full-blown colony. During the Napoleonic Wars, the British took the southern tip of Africa from the Dutch farmers known as Boers and established Cape Colony, which many British continued to see as the only hope for African civilization. In 1836 the Boers moved north in their Great Trek to escape British control and create their own states in the Transvaal. This brought them – and later the British – into head-on clashes with native tribesmen, notably the Zulu.

There can be no doubt that the period after 1815 saw a scramble for empire as the benefits were deemed to be huge. Untold natural resources lay waiting to be exploited by Europeans: grain, tea, sugar, jute, meat, copra, cotton, silk, gold, diamonds, tin, copper, rubber, wool, oil and much more were prize commodities representing millions in the increasingly global economy. Britain's position after the overthrow of Napoleon was unique. The Russian, Austro-Hungarian and Ottoman empires were largely or totally land-locked. France still had overseas possessions, but had just been defeated and would be watched very carefully. So had Spain, but by the nineteenth century that country was a spent force, her *sieclo d'oro* ('golden century') far behind her. The list of acquisitions by Britain, almost all in Samuel Baker's lifetime, is astonishing. Britain by force and treaty acquired Singapore in 1819, Malacca in 1824, Hong Kong in 1842, Natal in 1843, Lower Burma in 1852 and Lagos in 1861, and claimed sovereignty over Australia and New Zealand by 1840. The American president Monroe famously warned Europeans not to meddle in his country's affairs in 1823, but the British already had Canada and, until 1846, Oregon too.

Any British atlas printed in the second half of the nineteenth century showed Britain and her empire in red (in practice, usually pink) and it was impressive. One in my own possession dated 1886 has interminable lists of produce exported by Britain to the colonies and the returning raw materials from them. A proud previous owner has written in by hand at least as many more.

It was not difficult to find supporters for British imperialism, long before Baker and Kipling. In 1849 Thomas Carlyle wrote in the journal *Horoscope*: 'Our little isle is grown too narrow for us; but the world is wide enough yet for another six thousand years .... What a future; wide as the world, if we have the heart and heroism for it – which, by Heaven's blessing, we shall.' An unlikely advocate was the artist, critic and environmentalist John Ruskin. Addressing Oxford University in February 1870, he said:

> This is what [England] must do or perish; she must found colonies as fast and as far as she is able, formed of her most energetic and worthiest men – seizing every piece of fruitful waste ground she can set her foot on and there teaching these her colonists that ... their first aim is to be to advance the power of England by land and sea.[6]

Soon after Baker was dead, Thomas Hodgson wrote in *The Aboriginal Friend* (July 1896): 'It was the mission of the Anglo-Saxon race to penetrate into every part of the world and to help in the great work of civilization.'

There were, of course, critics in equal number and they are in the ascendancy today. Thomas Fowell Buxton, speaking in the Commons in 1837, the year that Victoria became queen and when Samuel Baker was still at school, could almost have invented political correctness:

> Too often, [the natives'] territory has been usurped, their property seized, their numbers diminished, their character debased, the spread of religion impeded. European vices and diseases have been introduced among them and they have been familiarized with the use of our most potent instruments for the subtle or violent destruction of human life viz. brandy and gunpowder.[7]

The previous year, Charles Darwin, on board the *Beagle* in the South Seas, came to the same conclusion: 'Wherever the European has trod, death seems to pursue the aboriginal. We may look to the wide extent of the Americas, Polynesia, the Cape of Good Hope and Australia and we find the same result.'[8]

By the time Samuel Baker left Ceylon, the brilliant economist/businessman Richard Cobden had economic objections to imperialism: 'The idea of defending, as integral parts of our empire, countries 10,000 miles off, like Australia, which neither pay a shilling to our revenue ... nor afford us any exclusive trade ... is about as quixotic a specimen of national folly as was ever exhibited.'[9] What most opponents of imperialism fixed on was the arrogance of the British in their natural presumption that their way of life was superior, that God was not only an Englishman, but probably a public schoolboy. 'The white man must rule,' wrote Lord Milner in March 1903, 'because he is elevated by many, many steps above the black man: steps which it will take the latter centuries to climb and which it is quite possible that the vast bulk of the black population may never be able to climb at all.'[10]

Today, this is seen as overt racism, and it is difficult to look at it any other way. The French aristocrat Arthur de Gobineau had gone further in 1855:

Human history is like an immense tapestry ... The two most inferior varieties of the human species, the black and yellow races, are the crude foundation, the cotton and the wool, which the secondary families of the white race make supple by adding their silk; while the Aryan group, circling its finer threads through the noble generation, designs on its surface a dazzling masterpiece of arabesques in silver and gold.[11]

The lofty (and liberal) *Edinburgh Review* had a different slant:

It is a noble work to plant the foot of England and extend her sceptre by the banks of streams unnamed and over regions yet unknown – and to conquer, not by the tyrannous subjugation of inferior races, but by the victories of mind over brute matter and blind mechanical obstacles. A yet nobler work is to diffuse over a new created world the laws of Alfred, the language of Shakespeare and the Christian religion, the last great heritage of man.[12]

In the 1860s the *Anthropological Review* tended to agree: 'They [natives] are beardless children whose life is a task and whose chief virtue consists in unquestioning obedience.'[13] That arch-hypocrite[14] Henry Labouchere MP parodied one of the great Christian hymns when he wrote:

Onward, Christian soldiers!
On to heathen lands!
Prayer-books in your pockets!
Rifles in your hands!
Take the glorious tidings
Where trade can be won,
Spread the peaceful gospel –
With a Maxim gun![15]

The Maxim gun was simply a quick-firing deliverer of the gunpowder that Buxton had warned about fifty years earlier.

The novelist Joseph Conrad had no doubt about imperialism. In *Heart of Darkness* (1902) he wrote:

It was just robbing with violence, aggravated murder on a great scale and men going at it blind – as is proper for those who tackle darkness. The conquest of the earth, which mostly means the taking it away from those who have a different complexion or slightly flatter noses than ourselves, is not a pretty thing when you look at it too much. What redeems it is the idea only.

George Bernard Shaw had something to say (when did he not?) about those ideas too: 'As the great champion of freedom and national independence, he [the Imperialist] conquers and annexes half the world and calls it Colonisation ... He does everything on principle. He fights you on patriotic principles; he robs you on business principles; he enslaves you on imperial principles.'[16]

How can we explain British imperialism? The British have long prided themselves on their sense of fair play; British justice and integrity were renowned throughout the world. What was more natural than that they should bestow these qualities on the rest of the world?[17] Part of the answer to the complexity of the imperial question lies in the unconscious racism that we have discussed already. Men such as Baker would simply not have understood that the British way of life could be bettered – and therefore it could not be criticized. Rather as Winston Churchill famously described democracy as the worst system of government in the world except all the others, so British imperialism occupied a similar position. The other element in all this, encapsulated by R.J. Lowe's *The Reluctant Imperialists* (1967), is that the British empire was a sporadic, piece-meal and unplanned event. 'We seem, as it were,' said Sir John Seeley, 'to have conquered and peopled half the world in a fit of absence of mind.'[18]

We shall examine Baker's views on Africa later, but like all men with experience at the rock face, he did not share the dewy-eyed optimism of the do-gooders at home. When Sir Bartle Frere and Lord Chelmsford between them engineered a war against the Zulu, William Gladstone, leader of the Liberal opposition, waxed lyrical about the 'noble savage', completely ignoring the fact that Cetewayo, the Zulu king, had come to power by murdering members of his own family. Baker wished that:

> The black sympathisers in England could see Africa's innermost heart as I do; much of their sympathies would subside. Human nature when viewed in its crude state as pictured amongst African savages is quite on a level with that of the brute and not to be compared with the noble character of the dog.[19]

Today's liberals support self-determination and wring their hands in helplessness when Africa throws up an Idi Amin or a Robert Mugabe. Samuel Baker would have recognized both these despots very readily – every African king he met behaved likewise. One of the 'civilizing' effects of British imperialism was the work of missionaries. Again, we shall consider the African experience later, but at the end of his time in Ceylon (1855) Baker returned to the notion of the 'White Man's Burden': 'Here lies [Britain's] responsibility. The conquered nations are in her hands; they have been subject to her for half a century, but they know neither her language nor her religion.'

Baker confessed to some confusion in the fact that Britain was a Christian, in fact Protestant, state, sending its missionaries throughout the world, yet at the same time protecting Buddhism in Ceylon:

'We even stretched the point so far as to place a British sentinel on guard at the Buddhist temple in Kandy, as though in mockery of our Protestant church a hundred paces distant.'[20]

He was equally critical of the education brought by his own people. Sinhalese children were crammed with 'useless nonsense' which was not only irrelevant to them, but gave them expectations they could not possibly hope to match in adult life. And he was scathing on the mismatch of colonial and home-grown education: 'It is absurd to hear the arguments in favour of mathematics, geography etc. for the native children, when a large proportion of our own population in Great Britain can neither read nor write.'[21]

Vitally, Baker believed, all nations should learn English because 'it lessens the distance between the white man and the black'. This sounds like a nod in the direction of equality, but in fact it was merely a prerequisite to the natives' acquisition of English customs and ideas, which were so naturally superior that Baker does not have to say so. It was too late for the adults – 'they must be abandoned like the barren fig tree'. It was the 'young shoots' that needed the attention of teachers. When in Ceylon, Baker was asked by the locals to establish a school for them. One of the headmen of a village 12 miles from Baker's settlement at Newera Ellia said of his own people, 'They are growing up as ignorant as our young buffaloes.'

The sort of school that Baker had in mind was one like the Reverend Thurston had recently set up at Colombo. It was an industrial school, the forerunner of the technical colleges of the early twentieth century, where pupils learned a trade, be it weaving or tapioca-growing. There should be a school like this for every hundred boys (Baker, in keeping with Englishmen of his time and class, probably didn't consider girls worth educating), and there should be a tract of land attached to each building. 'By this means, in the course of a few years, we should secure an educated and useful population in lieu of the present indolent and degraded race ... Heathenism could not exist in such a state of affairs; it would die out.'[22]

Ironically, what Baker was proposing was self-sufficiency on a limited industrial scale for India. When Mohandas K. Gandhi advocated an extension of this towards the end of Baker's life, he was ignored and finally victimized by the British, who insisted that Indians bought British manufactured goods instead. And neither the half-naked fakir in a loincloth[23] nor any other leader saw any role for Christianity in the new India. Perhaps it is not surprising – as Baker himself said: 'I have met many strange things during my journeys, but I never recollect having met a missionary.'

It was Rudyard Kipling who summed up the infuriating complexity of the British imperialist. Five years after Samuel Baker died, he wrote about another school, that set up by Kitchener, the victor of Omdurman, in the Sudan, which Baker would have known well:

> Knowing that ye are forfeit by battle and have no right to live,
> He begs for money to bring you learning – and all the English give.
> It is their treasure – it is their pleasure – thus are their hearts inclined;
> For Allah created the English mad – the maddest of all mankind.

The following year he wrote (ironically of the Philippines and American expansionism there):

> Take up the White Man's burden –
> Send forth the best ye breed –
> Go bind your sons to exile
> To serve your captives' needs;
> To wait in heavy harness
> On fluttered folk and wild –
> Your new-caught, sullen peoples,
> Half devil and half child.

The devils, the children, the burden itself: these were the experiences of one of the best that England bred – Samuel White Baker.

Chapter 2

The Bakers' Half-Dozen

Like many families that reached eminence in the nineteenth century, the Bakers' forebears had been among those 'self-made men' to prosper under the Tudors. The upheavals of the mid-fifteenth century known as the Wars of the Roses had decimated the aristocracy – and they also taught the new royal dynasty to distrust those who were left. Accordingly, new men replaced the old and something approaching a meritocracy emerged briefly by the early sixteenth century.

Sir John Baker, of Sissinghurst, Kent, must have made an impression. A product, as many politicians of the next two centuries would be, of the London Inns of Court, he became attorney-general and recorder of the capital, both senior law positions. He gravitated to the post of chancellor of the Exchequer under Henry VIII and speaker of the Commons under Mary.

These were difficult years in government. The impact of the Reformation from Martin Luther's 'Germany' meant that England was affected, like all other European states, by the threat of Protestantism. Henry VIII's break with Rome and the dissolution of the monasteries proved to be nails in the Catholic coffin, and during Baker's time at the Exchequer the new king, Edward, was a minor and under the thumb of a Protestant regent – 'Protector' Somerset. The boy-king's death at the age of 16, however, saw a reversal. The staunch Catholic Mary became queen, executed Somerset and turned the Protestant regime on its head. As the smoke of burning martyrs blew across London from Smithfield, parliament was expected to ratify all the whims of these monarchs.

As Speaker, John Baker's job was a particularly difficult one. He was nominally the monarch's eyes and ears in the Commons, but the religious see-saw of fifteen years had led to a growing sense of alienation between Mary and her parliament. This would continue under her sister, Elizabeth, and rumble into open defiance and eventually civil war under the first two Stuarts. It was perhaps to explain some of this that Sir Richard Baker wrote *The Chronicle of the Kings of England*, republished for the third time in 1660 in a country grateful for the restoration of monarchy and longing for a period of stability.

The branch of the Baker family from which Samuel descended held estates near Poole in Dorset and, not surprisingly in a coastal town, had links with the navy. Three generations of Bakers had served in the Royal Navy, from its reinstitution in 1660 to the time that the family's colourful member Valentine Baker, Samuel Baker's grandfather, hit the headlines.

In 1775 war broke out between Britain and her thirteen colonies in America. A sordid squabble over trade and the payment of taxes was made somehow noble by the Virginian lawyer Thomas Jefferson the following year, when he wrote (lifting heavily from the English philosopher John Locke) the Declaration of Independence. That year saw Valentine Baker resign his commission, but that meant that he could work freelance for the British as commander of an 18-gun sloop, the *Caesar* (previously called the *Black Joke*), as a privateer, carrying letters of marque. Well established under Elizabeth, privateers were little more than pirates, but they worked in practice under government orders – a government that would of course deny any knowledge of a ship's existence if things went wrong.

Valentine Baker found fame in 1782. In practice the war in the Americas was over – General Cornwallis's surrender at Yorktown the previous year marked the end of actual hostilities. But a major reason for British defeat was the fact that France, Spain and Holland had all declared war on her on behalf of the American colonies. So when the *Caesar* saw the sails of a 32-gun French frigate in the Channel, Baker gave chase. It was a dogged fight and one the outgunned *Caesar* should have lost, but in fact the French commander, his ship smashed and leaking, struck his colours – in effect, surrendered. The *Caesar* was damaged too, and in the chaos of battle the Frenchman rehoisted her flag and made for home. Another British man-of-war easily overtook the crippled vessel and towed her in to

Portsmouth, where the *Caesar* was already undergoing repairs. The French captain, embarrassed at his deceptive behaviour in the face of the enemy, shot himself.

Perhaps there was a need for some good news at the end of a mismanaged and disappointing war, and Valentine Baker became an instant hero. The citizens of Bristol, the richest slave port in the world before the trade's abolition in 1807, showered riches and honours on him. As a privateer Baker had helped himself to a considerable amount of prize money, and as well as fitting out a profitable merchant fleet out of Bristol, he invested in property in Jamaica and Mauritius.

The Baker link with the wild and foreign climes really dates from this period. Britain may have lost America, but she was still the most formidable imperial power in the world after France, and after 1815 had no rivals at all. Men with vision, men with money, men with a wanderlust, bought plantations and farms in the world's farthest corners and brought a little bit of British civilization to them.

Of Valentine's nine children, only one, Samuel, raised a family that lived to adulthood. The great serial killers of the nineteenth century – cholera, typhoid, typhus fever – lay in the years ahead, but smallpox, tuberculosis, diphtheria and a host of other incurable ailments swept away children like chaff at harvest time, irrespective of social class. Samuel was sent, in the year of Waterloo, to manage the family estates in Jamaica. He obviously had no clear idea why he was going. Bouncing about in a sailing packet on the three-month journey, he wrote in his diary that he was 'an unlucky young dog taking the voyage, he hardly knew why, but imagined it may be partly to keep him from an idle winter and to strengthen a sickly constitution'.[1] There may be some truth in both these judgements. Samuel may well have been wealthy enough to spend many idle winters and that did not square with the Protestant work ethic to which his family clearly subscribed. The climate of the West Indies (actually potentially lethal) was believed to be a panacea for many problems, rather as Switzerland was later in the century.

Putting in to Funchal en route, Baker visited a convent where a pretty nun confided that she had once been kissed by a friar. He watched the sunset with her and murmured, 'Can such a creature as an atheist exist?'[2]

On arrival in the West Indies, Baker found the scenery 'sublime'. A major surprise in store for Samuel was the condition of the slaves in his father's plantation. The average cost of an adult male slave was $40 in the 1790s, and this was rising after 1815. The trade itself had been abolished eight years earlier by a parliament suddenly embarrassed by William Wilberforce and undergoing one of its fits of morality. Samuel Baker wrote: 'Mr Wilberforce should certainly be sent to Jamaica to witness the Christmas gambols of these poor slaves. For ten successive nights I could scarcely sleep for the infernal noises of the "enslaved mortals".'[3] A modern complaint might be that the Afro-Caribbeans should not have been forced to adopt an alien religion in the first place, no matter how much they enjoyed it. The 'peculiar institution' of slavery was finally abolished in 1833, and, as slave owners, the Bakers duly received huge compensation for their loss.

Samuel had the same business sense as his father, and on his return from the West Indies divided his time between London, rapidly becoming the largest port in the world, and Ridgeway Oaks, the estate that became his by marriage to Mary, daughter of Thomas Dobson of Enfield. The second of the couple's five sons, christened Samuel White, was delivered in the family's London house in Whitehall Yard, on 8 June 1821. A hero was born.

The world into which Baker was born was in a state of flux. Months before, an ugly crowd had roared its disapproval as a masked headsman decapitated Arthur Thistlewood and his Cato Street conspirators after their abortive attempt to assassinate the Cabinet. A still uglier mob had gone on the rampage even more recently in support of England's 'injured queen', Caroline of Brunswick, the estranged wife of the new king, George IV. She died when Baker was three months old, after a three-week illness diagnosed as 'acute inflammation of the bowels'. Half of London mourned her; the other half cheered. We do not know where the Baker family's loyalties lay.

What we can be sure of is that had Samuel been older at the time he would have cheered the sight – for the last time in British history – of the king's champion, armed cap-à-pie in Elizabethan armour, throwing down his gauntlet at the coronation of the otherwise unlovely George IV. All his life, Samuel White Baker approved of such romantic gestures and made a few of them himself.

In the London of his birth, Thomas De Quincey published *Confessions of an English Opium-Eater*; the new Bank of England, thirty years in the building, was finally opened in Threadneedle Street; and an unknown scientist, Michael Faraday, built an electric motor. The decade which was the first of Baker's life was a time of unprecedented expansion. As the superpowers of Europe – Russia, Austro-Hungary and France – consolidated their grip on their land empires and where possible enlarged them, Britain went in a different direction, towards an overseas empire and the domination of world trade.

For complex reasons, the country had emerged by the 1820s as the foremost manufacturing economy in the world. Twenty years later, German visitors were astonished by the size of British factories and the extent of production. It was not by accident that Karl Marx and Friedrich Engels based their socialist principles in the richest country in the world. The 'workshop of the world' was the background to the success of the Baker family. It was because of this that Baker himself had a leisurely life as a child when his working-class contemporaries were already climbing under cotton machines at seven years of age, the factory Acts having had little effect on the systematic abuse of generations. With the dynamic William Huskisson at the Board of Trade from 1822, commerce was opened with the new South American republics that Britain had done so much to create. North America, not yet in a position to forge its own industrial revolution, had no choice but to trade with Britain.

The Bakers' 'half-dozen' were all born in this decade. Thomas was the first, but was dead by 1832. After Samuel came John, who would remain closest to his brother, then Valentine and James. John would become one of the first tea planters in Ceylon. Valentine would become Baker Pasha, a distinguished soldier and the centre of one of the most celebrated scandals of the century. James, also a soldier, would emigrate to Canada and become minister of education in British Columbia. There were three daughters, Mary, Ann and Ellen, described by Dorothy Middleton as 'women of charm and personality', and the whole brood were close as children and remained so into adulthood. 'This strong family feeling was

Sam Baker's anchor,' Middleton believed; 'without it, he might have led a less useful life and have been a less happy man. It was this firm foundation on which he built his castles in the air.'[4]

The family moved regularly between the Whitehall Yard town house, near the Thames and within a stone's throw of the great government offices of state, and Ridgeway Oaks. Enfield was only 12 miles away, but before the coming of the railway the journey would have been undertaken by pony and trap or a larger gig for the whole family. The town was bisected by the New River and boasted the twelfth-century church of St Andrew, as well as the ruins of the palace built by Edward VI when John Baker was his chancellor of the Exchequer. The King and Tinker inn had associations with James I, who hunted frequently in the nearby Chase, and the grammar school had been founded in 1537.

In common with his siblings, Samuel was taught by his mother. The usual pattern for families of this social standing was that a nanny would cope with the babies, toddlers and small children up to the age of seven, and then a governess or tutor would be employed. Of the boy's education in his early years, we know little. 'Geography was his delight,' wrote a contemporary many years later, 'and as a mere baby he had learned the names of all the countries then known and had acquired some knowledge of their capitals and their special characteristics.'[5] Science also fascinated Samuel. With his close-knit siblings in tow, he made collections of bugs, birds' eggs, plants, *anything* in fact which he found interesting or could not explain. When puppies or kittens on the Ridgeway estate were drowned – which was routine – he would try to resuscitate them.[6] When that failed, he buried them with almost military solemnity. According to family legend, he once placed his sister Ann in a flower bed up to her neck, to see if she would grow faster.

Perhaps because of this rather dangerous bent towards practical experimental science, Samuel was packed off to a school in Rottingdean, near Brighton. Now associated with the 'poet of empire', Rudyard Kipling, who lived there at Bateman's, the village was nondescript in Baker's day, and there are no records of the school available. By definition, it was a boarding school and one of dozens of private establishments springing up all over the country to cater for a rising middle class that could not afford the fees of, or were suspicious of, the similarly burgeoning public schools. A description of the 10-year-old Samuel was written many years later:

> He was of the Saxon type, a noble-looking boy, with very fair complexion, light hair and fearless blue eyes. He was enterprising, mischievous, forever getting into scrapes ... but he was never known to tell a lie nor to do a mean thing ... a plucky little fellow, ready to fight much bigger boys than himself on the slightest charge of homesickness or for any infringement of his rights.[7]

This was the time that one of the century's greatest headmasters, Thomas Arnold at Rugby, was turning out 'Christian gentlemen' exactly in the Baker mould. And despite the fact that the education Samuel received at Rottingdean was probably fairly basic, we know that he could write. A letter written from the school in March 1832 testifies to the scientific experiments – including dangerous ones with gunpowder – he was carrying out at home in the holidays:

> My dear Aunt ... Tell me in your next letter whether you forgot to take the pieces of metal that I found with a piece of flint in the middle to London, because since you left us I have found several bits of the same sort in the house, which I suppose had been broken off the same lump.[8]

That was the year that Samuel's brother Thomas died, leaving him the eldest in the family. It was also the year when the country convulsed in potential revolution over the passage of the Whigs' Reform Bill, doubling the size of the electorate and signalling the end of civilization to reactionary diehards such as the Duke of Wellington.

A year later, the Baker family moved from the Ridgeway to Highnam Court, near Gloucester. The estate belonged to the Guise family, and the Bakers took out a lease on it. The park, stocked with deer, ran to 56 acres, with a further 2,000 acres of open country beyond that. The impressive Georgian house still stands, the gardens open to the public. Here, Baker developed his passion for hunting and for wildlife which would stay with him all his life. The red deer in the nearby Forest of Dean were the property of the crown, but Baker the young naturalist contented himself with writing notes on them and trying to measure the stags' antlers.

The move necessitated a further change of school. Baker was now 13, traditionally the age for boys to move from a preparatory to a public school. Instead, he attended as a day boy Gloucester School, near the city's medieval cathedral, together with his brothers John and Valentine. Of his time there, Baker wrote: 'I believe that I was the only boy who never received corporal punishment, an exception amongst 96 individuals. The solitary exception of myself from the cane or birch was not the result of any superior merit on my part; I was only a size too big and too strong.' He also wrote, 'My reminiscences of the College School are not agreeable.'[9] By the time he was 17 he had reached his 5 feet 10 inches, with a stockiness that matched; as a middle-aged man he reached 15 stone. His build helped him lay out a local Gloucester bully with a single punch.

Again, not following the traditional educational path, certain options lay before Baker at this stage. It was 1837, the year that his almost exact contemporary, Victoria, became queen. The traditional 'gap year' of the grand tour in which young gentlemen soaked up the classical sights and fleshpots of Europe was a thing of the past. Benjamin Disraeli, determined to make himself an English gentleman, had gone six years earlier and merely became a laughing stock as a result. The universities of Oxford, Cambridge and newly created London were an expensive option, but Baker hardly showed the aptitude for scholarly pursuits. Traditionally, eldest sons followed their fathers in whatever calling they followed, and this seemed Baker's destiny. First, though, his education had to be brought up to scratch. Already an expert in firearms (he had a gun made to his own specifications at the age of 19), he lacked other talents. His father found a private tutor for the boy – H.P. Dunster, the curate of Tottenham (then still a marshy village separate from London) – not that much older than Baker himself. 'He was at that time [1838],' wrote Dunster, 'a strong, well-made lad with a very gentlemanly bearing, a florid complexion, bright auburn hair and an open, honest countenance, full of life and animal spirits.'[10]

Baker was average in Latin – he and Dunster read Caesar and Livy together – but he knew no Greek at all. The classics of course may have had no obvious relevance to nineteenth-century life, but they were seen as the cornerstone of civilization and the hallmark of a gentleman. Baker took to Xenophon like a duck to water, and he immersed himself in Dunster's father's huge library. His favourites were Madden's *Travels*, focusing on the West Indies, and Balzoni's *Travels in Egypt and Nubia*, both books bestsellers in an age when travelogues were all the rage. Borrowing heavily from Tottenham's excellent circulating library – itself a relatively new phenomenon – Baker continued his scientific experiments with Dunster and went shooting with the curate's spaniel on the Tottenham marshes, when he wasn't perfecting his swimming skills in the local river.

It had probably been in their father's mind all along that Samuel and John should both go to Mauritius to run the estates there, and to that end Samuel should follow a business course. Such courses, being beneath the dignity of a scholar, were offered by no English university, so Samuel was sent to Frankfurt to learn at the elbow of a master, the banker Behrens. It does not say much for English education that so many influential people were taught on the continent. Arthur Wellesley, the Duke of Wellington, was sent to Angers in France because there were no military academies available in England. Florence Nightingale learned her skills in Germany because nowhere in England trained nurses.

Frankfurt-am-Main was the traditional crowning place of medieval German emperors, and from 1815 the capital of the confederation that would become a united Germany by 1871. In Baker's time it was the commercial and political capital which would not be eclipsed by Berlin until the turn of the century. Baker would have known the huge rambling Roemer, the town hall and the Kaisersaal, the great banqueting hall. He would also have been familiar with the city's medieval cathedrals and churches, although St Paul's was still being built while he was there. The schools were the envy of all the German states and beyond, and no doubt it was this reputation that impressed Baker senior to send his son there.

Baker spent eighteen months in Frankfurt, showing his ability in languages by learning to speak and write fluent German. He also found time to hunt boar in the local forests. His homecoming to London, however, must have been anti-climactic. As a clerk scratching away with a quill pen on the high, upright desk in his father's

Fenchurch Street offices, he was utterly bored. The young man was itching for adventure – perhaps his time in Germany had given him the taste for travel that never left him. It was 1840. Rowland Hill introduced his black one penny stamp to a dubious public. Charles Green announced to a far more dubious public that he intended to float across the Channel in a balloon. For those already bored by gin, whisky and conventional drinks, the Schweppes company of London added quinine and sugar to its recipe and produced tonic water, and restaurateur James Pimm produced his Number One for jaded palettes.

Further afield, Britain, ever the 'reluctant imperialist', annexed New Zealand, granting certain rights to the native Maori. In part, this happened for a European reason; if Britain had not annexed New Zealand, France – the old enemy – would have. Such geopolitics would shape the future for Samuel White Baker.

Chapter 3

Newera Ellia

The summer of 1843 saw Charles Napier, beard to his waist and sunglasses strapped to his solar topi, take the Indian province of Scinde, an area about the size of Wales. It was one of the many additions to empire that took place during Samuel Baker's lifetime.

But that summer he may have been too busy to notice. On 3 August he and his brother John married Henrietta and Elizabeth, respectively, daughters of the Reverend Charles Martin, vicar of Maisemore, the parish that skirted the Highnam estate. The girls' little sister Charlotte was a bridesmaid. Samuel was 22 and John 21 when the double ceremony took place at the parish church. It was followed by a joint honeymoon in Clifton, a village on the edge of Bristol. Isambard Kingdom Brunel's famous suspension bridge was twenty years in the future and the place, with its gorge and the lofty rocks of St Vincent, was famous for its hot springs and pump room.

The tight family unit of sisters paired with brothers was to go out to Mauritius to manage Fairfund, the Baker estates there, which was seen as fitting work for the eldest boys and probably their father's plan all along. John and Elizabeth sailed on the 100-ton *Jack* around the Cape. Before the opening of the Suez Canal in 1869, there were two routes into the Indian Ocean; the sea voyage, of which *Jack* underwent part, took eight months to reach the subcontinent. The alternative overland way was by ship to Port Said and then across the desert by camel and donkey train to the Red Sea, to join a second ship.

Baker and Henrietta stayed at Highnam, and it was here a year after the wedding that their first child was born, christened Charles Martin after his maternal grandfather. By the time the family set sail, Henrietta was pregnant again.[1] Undertaking a four- or five-month journey by sea at such a time was a risk the Bakers thought worth taking.

Years later, Mark Twain wrote of Mauritius: 'From one citizen you gather the idea that Mauritius was made first, and then Heaven, and that Heaven was copied after Mauritius. Another one tells you that this is an exaggeration.'[2] The latter version would almost certainly have been the view of Samuel Baker. The island is part of the Mascarene archipelago, the result of volcanic upheaval between 8 and 10 million years ago. It lies 2,300 miles from the Cape and has an area of 720 square miles. It is a rugged and beautiful island, surrounded by coral reefs with fertile valleys and majestic mountains, the highest being the Piton de la Petite Rivière Noire, at 2,717 feet. The climate is tropical, fanned by the south-east trade winds. The winters are dry and warm, extending from May to November, and the summers hot and wet with a heavy rainfall. It was not a healthy place, and the damp may well have contributed to the death of little Charles Martin, early in 1845.

The Arabs had known Mauritius since the tenth century, but the first Europeans to settle there were the Portuguese, who landed in 1507 in the wake of Vasco da Gama's rounding of the Cape of Good Hope. Since the Portuguese target, like that of every other trading nation, was India, they merely left a base and moved on, leaving the place open to the Dutch. In 1598 a cyclone, to which the area is prone, blew three ships of the second fleet off course, and they found the island by chance, claiming it for Maurice of Nassau, Stadtholder of the United Provinces, which was then emerging as a separate breakaway state from Spain's Holy Roman Empire. The first permanent settlement on Maurice's Island was set up in 1638.

The adverse weather conditions and lack of game saw the little colony collapse, and the island was deserted by 1715 when the French occupied it as Île de France. The eighteenth century saw a huge growth of imperial expansion for both France and Britain, but the wars fought between those powers saw the decline of one and the rise of the other, especially in overseas colonial terms. Under the French, for the best part of a century, Mauritius became prosperous. African slaves could easily be imported to the sugar plantations, and all Europe, it seemed, wanted sugar as a staple ingredient in the coffee houses which were the social centres of the European capitals.

When war broke out again between Britain and France in 1793, the prime minister, William Pitt, was determined to fight a 'blue water' war as his father, the Earl of Chatham, had; in other words, a war fought in the colonies. Though most of Napoleon Bonaparte's campaigns were centred firmly in Europe itself, there were overseas clashes. The French used Mauritius as a base to attack passing British ships, and the skirmish off Grand Port was the only French naval victory over the British in the entire twenty-two years of war. It made little difference. On 3 December 1810 the French garrison formally surrendered to the British at Cap Malheureuse, and the island effectively became British.

The overthrow of Bonaparte and the subsequent treaties agreed at the Congress of Vienna saw what turned out to be an unsatisfactory solution in respect of Mauritius. The name Île de France vanished and the island was officially a crown colony, run by a succession of British governors, but the French landowners were allowed to keep their estates, income, language and law (the Code Napoléon).

By the time the Bakers arrived, the island's population must have been an odd mix indeed. There were the British, like the Bakers themselves, at Fairfund, still the old enemy, who had as little to do with the governor as possible, and the Creoles, the half-French, half-Mauritian result of a century of interbreeding. To add to the complexity, the recent abolition of slavery meant that labour on the Bakers' plantation was carried out largely by workers drafted in from India. The racial and religious tensions must have been palpable – French Catholics and British Protestants attempting to live alongside Muslims, Hindus, perhaps even the odd Sikh. It did not make for an easy life, but it probably gave Samuel Baker invaluable experience in handling natives in difficult situations.

What struck Baker most forcefully, as a keen hunter and observer of wildlife already, was the lack of fauna on Mauritius. The island's isolation meant that many unique examples of life flourished there, but the 1840s was perhaps a little early for that notion to be understood by anyone. The island's most famous native, the flightless dodo, was very rare by the late seventeenth century, and definitely extinct by 1700, wiped out by hunters in just 100 years from their first contact. There were macaques, which fed on crabs and 'flying fox' fruit bats. The birds included the grey white-eye, the kestrel and the parakeet, all now dangerously close to extinction. Geckos and boa constrictors were the most common of the reptiles, but it is probable that the last of the giant tortoises had died out before the Bakers arrived.

In June 1845, only months after the death of little Charles, Henrietta gave birth to a second son, John Lindsay Sloane. Perhaps it was some consolation. The consolation for Baker was different – 'It was in the year 1845 that the spirit of wandering allured me towards Ceylon.' He had been reading *Blackwood's Magazine* with its exciting accounts of elephant hunting and was determined to see the place for himself. He went to reconnoitre, leaving his family at Fairfund under the care of John, and sailed the 2,500 miles across the Indian Ocean.

Unlike Mauritius, Ceylon had a long recorded history, and its climate and fauna were much more to Baker's taste. Buddhist by the third century BC, the island was constantly threatened by powerful invading princes from India and fought over by Lankan and Tamil tribes for centuries. The Portuguese landed in 1505, and established an outpost or 'factory' at Colombo twelve years later. Constantly at loggerheads with the Sinhalese, the Portuguese were probably grateful to give way to the Dutch by 1658. In the 1790s, when the Low Countries were French allies, the British captured the Sinhalese Dutch outposts, and the coastal regions were formally ceded to Britain in 1802. By 1815 the central province of Kandy fell to the British, and the whole island became, like Mauritius, a crown colony.

The pear-shaped island is geologically an extension of India's Deccan plateau, with a mountainous mass to the south. The highest peak is Pedrotallagalla, at 8,294 feet, and the Mahaweli Ganga is the longest river, snaking north-east 206 miles to the sea. Baker found that the climate was tropical, but, unlike Mauritius, much affected by the monsoon. This varies over the island: the heaviest rains fall in the south-west between June and October, but in the north-east the wet season runs from November to December.

A gazetteer of the 1950s, by which time the British had recently pulled out, ushering in decades of civil war, lists the island's exports. Precious stones were found in the old crystalline rocks in the interior and graphite (plumbago) abounded. Iron ore, china clay, rubies and opals existed in limited quantities, and the towns produced leather goods, glass and pottery. Tea was exported, as was rubber, cinnamon, areca nuts and copra. What is not listed is the substance that Baker looked upon as a sound investment for his and Henrietta's future – coffee.

Many of the men Baker met on his visit to Ceylon were coffee planters, and he formed very clear opinions of them; 'a coffee estate is not infrequently abused for not paying – when it is worked with borrowed capital, at a high rate of interest, under questionable superintendence ... a rapid fortune can never be made by working a coffee estate'.[3] His father's and Herr Behrens' training had worked; Baker was aware of the hazards. But a man with his own capital and a grasp of management, and prepared to put personal work in, had it made.

At first Baker was not impressed by the seaport of Colombo. It was at least a century behind Mauritius, the laid-back harbour a poor second to the bustling Port Louis on the smaller island. The guns on the fort ramparts looked unfireable, the garrison 'parboiled' under the scorching sun. Everybody sauntered rather than walked, and the bullock carts were virtually stationary. Port Louis's shops bristled with goods, where everything from a needle to a crowbar could be bought. Colombo had almost no shops. Baker took a room at the Royal or Seager's Hotel, which was white-painted and airy, but hardly comfortable.

Refreshed with tiffin, he hired a carriage which reminded him of a hearse back home, and visited the celebrated Cinnamon Gardens he had heard so much about – 'What fairy-like pleasure-grounds have we fondly anticipated! What perfumes of spices ...' The reality? 'A vast area of scrubby, low jungle' – something else to add to the 'disappointment of a visitor to Colombo'. Among others, he passed what he thought was a beautiful woman carrying a pitcher; she turned out to have a beard and be a sneak-thief. When he asked two white planters about 'sport' in the area – which, to Baker, meant hunting – they spoke languidly about the Galle Face racecourse. As for elephants, there may have been a few, 'but you never see them'.[4]

A weaker man might have given up and gone home, but Baker was not to be deterred. He knew that the 15th Foot were stationed in Ceylon and looked up an old friend of his from Gloucestershire,

Lieutenant de Montenac. Here was a man after his own heart, and he introduced Baker to the possibilities of the Ceylon hunt. Baker rented a 'good airy house in Colombo ... and the verandahs were soon strewed with jungle baskets, boxes, tent, gun-cases and all the paraphernalia of a shooting trip'.[5] Baker's obsession with hunting will be explored in subsequent chapters, but he enjoyed it so much and the prospect of a coffee plantation seemed so much better than the hard graft of Fairfund that he wrote to Henrietta, and later John and Elizabeth, to join him. But on the voyage tragedy struck Samuel and Henrietta for a second time, when in September 1846 Jane, their baby daughter, fell ill and died off the Maldives. She was buried at sea.

After a year in Ceylon, Baker himself fell ill. Many men were hit hard by fever on first arriving in the subcontinent – the term 'doolally' came from the British base at Deolali on the Indian mainland. Perhaps Baker was made of sterner stuff, but jungle fever (it may have been malaria) laid him low and he lost a considerable amount of weight. His doctor advised him to go north to the sanatorium in the high country at Newera Ellia. He was there for a fortnight and the food was terrible – 'it was a land of starvation', apart from beef-steak, black bread and potatoes – but the climate was superb and he was fit as a fiddle by the end of the two weeks.

Newera Ellia had been built by a former governor, Sir Edward Barnes, largely at his own expense, and the buildings included a barracks and officers' quarters. The governor's own stone-built property was said to have cost Barnes £8,000. After Barnes, however, the place became neglected and partly abandoned, and Baker was critical of his successors. 'In the present instance ... The movements of the governor (Sir G. Anderson) cannot carry much weight, as he does not move at all.'

Anderson's sole knowledge of Ceylon was the stretch of road between Colombo and Kandy. About 200 people lived at the hill-station, and Baker, with that characteristic optimism and forward planning which showed throughout his life, immediately had plans for them all. Good limestone lay only 5 miles away, and timber abounded on the mountainsides. The place cried out for cultivation: 'How often I have thought of the thousands of starving wretches at home, who might earn a comfortable livelihood!'[6] In his mind he cleared the forests and planted the corn, and built model dwellings for the community. He lay in his bed at night draining the marshes, building schools, hotels, a church.

It was the sudden collapse of the coffee market in 1847 that brought Newera Ellia into sharp focus. Samuel and John realized that land could now be bought for a fraction of the former price, but such a venture meant abandoning the Mauritian estates, and that meant a family discussion back home.

But 1848 was not a good year to travel. It was, with hindsight, the year of revolutions. Men and women manned the barricades in Paris and Vienna. Prince Metternich, the 'coachman of Europe' for nearly fifty years, was overthrown. Milan revolted against Austrian control and in Spain the Cortes (parliament) was suspended. Croatia, under the Hungarian nationalist Louis Kossuth, did its best to break up the Austro-Hungarian empire. In Rome, liberals took to the streets demanding reforms of the papacy. Everywhere, the world seemed on the brink of collapse.

The Bakers would have noticed a very different – and typically British – atmosphere on their return. In Ireland, William Smith O'Brien stood crying in a Dublin street because so few people had turned up for his planned revolution. And the last Chartist petition was delivered to parliament by a lone representative of the people in a carriage, because the weight of the paper was so immense. The 5 million names turned out to be under 2 million, with many repetitions. 'Flatnose' had signed it, as had 'Big Ears'; the Duke of Wellington's name was there, as was the queen's (four times). When the Chartists marched on London, they were outnumbered by the Peelers and special constables who steered them calmly to Kensington Common, where someone took the first ever photograph in Britain of a political event. It was all a huge anticlimax.

Samuel Baker senior had sold his estates at Lypiatt Park in Gloucestershire and moved to London because of his wife's increasing ill health. This made little sense in the scheme of things. By 1848 London was a dangerous place, with regular smogs and chronic outbreaks of cholera and typhoid. Edwin Chadwick's landmark reports on the condition of the poor and the state of interment in towns make grim reading, and although the poor suffered most, no one was exempt. No doubt the Bakers' business interests tied them to the capital, and Samuel senior would rather have his ailing wife with him.

The boys worked on their father and persuaded him that Ceylon had huge commercial advantages over Mauritius. Samuel junior in particular grew bored with London very quickly. He found the noise and bustle annoying, and made a nuisance of himself in gun-smiths, boring their proprietors with suggestions for modifications to their merchandise.

The plan for Newera Ellia was to create a little England at the hill-station, with the whole of Ceylon as Baker's shooting grounds. If this seems rather romantic and naive, it was a commonly held dream at the time. One of the likely causes of the Indian Mutiny in 1857 was the arrival of a new class of white officer, who brought his wife with him and set up little Leamingtons and Cheltenhams all over the subcontinent. These men created the Raj, which would last for another century. The almost feudal pattern of estate manage-ment that Baker had in mind had profound echoes elsewhere too. All his life he had known servants and deferential tenants, men who were still many years away from the vote (and their wives, longer still). Despite the empty noises of the Chartists and whatever was happening in Europe, this was the way of the world for men like Baker. And in the decade of revolutions, Benjamin Disraeli, with his Young England Conservatives in the Commons, may well have already been formulating his notion of Tory democracy, which was a vision of a reconstructed feudal society without the middle class.

Baker bought his land from the government at £1 per acre and set about building a town. John and his family would be part of the enterprise, of course, as would younger brother Valentine – although he probably already had his heart set on a military career, and his father would only let him go to Ceylon for a year. Samuel hired a bailiff (Mr Fowler), who came with wife and daughter, a blacksmith, a coachman (Henry Perkes) and eight others. Then he got himself some livestock: a half-bred Durham/Hereford bull, a Durham cow, three rams – Southdown, Leicester and Cotswold breeds – and a thoroughbred entire horse (stallion). So much for the farming animals; but, nearer to his heart, he took a pack of fox-hounds and Bran, his favourite greyhound.

Baker went ahead alone in August 1848 by the overland mail to prepare for the others, who embarked on the Green Company's *Earl of Hardwick* from the Port of London in September. An eyewitness watched them all leave Tilbury:

Young men and their wives, babies and nurses; the bailiff and his wife and daughter, the groom with the horses, the animals, two of every kind ... the cackle of poultry, the sad lowing of the cows, the plunging of the bull in mid-air as he was hauled up; and last of all, the pack of hounds, scrambling on board over the ship's side.[7]

Before they arrived, Baker used the time selecting the exact spot for the new settlement, comparing the event to the dove finding land after Noah's pilgrimage aboard the Ark. He rammed his walking stick into the earth 2½ miles from the sanatorium. The ground was ideal for the plough and not hemmed in by the mountains.

Rather like today's ex-pats who settle in summer climes because they enjoyed a pleasant holiday there, Baker quickly realized that there was a fly in the ointment. The monsoons hit in October, with incessant driving rain for days and nights, and the new lord of the manor had to pay exorbitant wages to his natives to work at all in weather like that. Eventually the monsoon was over and eighty men fell to work, clearing the forests with saws and axes. During all this building, Baker rented a house in Newera Ellia, and the rest of the party arrived safely in Colombo with the loss of only one hound.

In our jet age, we have forgotten the problems in simply travelling from A to B. Baker's cow weighed 13 hundredweight, and the walk to Newera Ellia would have killed her. The van he hired, which he was assured could carry an elephant, collapsed under the animal's weight, so there was nothing for it but to walk the entire menagerie, 10 miles a day, early in the morning and late in the evening to avoid the heat of the midday sun. Only the Bakers and their dogs could cope with that. The machinery was dragged on elephant carts, and an elephant waited at the entrance to the Newera Ellia pass to take the baggage and maids up.

Baker had brought out a new chaise, a family coach, from home, but the horses could not make the pass, so he sent Perkes the coachman back a few days later to bring it up. This proved a disaster:

Perkes was hardworking, but he also drank and went after anything in a skirt. A native brought a letter to Baker from his coachman the next day. The carriage and Walers (Australian horses) had tumbled down a precipice, and after an 80-foot drop, neither animals nor vehicle were in good repair. A neighbour 'is very kind', Perkes wrote, 'and has lent above a hundred niggers, but they ain't no more use than cats at liftin. Please Zor come and see whats to be done.'[8]

Baker does not record what he said to Perkes when they next met, but since both horses died we can be sure the language was fairly choice. Worse was to follow. The next day Baker received a letter telling him that his prize cow had died only 37 miles out of Colombo (Newera Ellia was 115 miles away). This was a blow as it ruled out the breeding of good cattle, which were to be a central part of the settlement's economy. Still, ill-advisedly, putting his faith in Perkes, Baker sent the coachman by elephant to haul the carriage from its ravine graveyard. Despite warnings from the mahout (elephant handler), Perkes insisted on driving his ankus (elephant goad) into the animal, forcing it along at a trot as though it were a cavalry horse. The elephant died the next day. Years later Baker could afford to be philosophical about these incidents – 'Mr Perkes was becoming an expensive man ... and he had the satisfaction of knowing he was one of the few men in the world who had ridden an elephant to death.'[9] Baker clearly tolerated such 'incorrigible scamps', though he could not understand Perkes's phenomenal success – despite the loss of an eye to a kick from a horse years before – with the maidservants.

There were now 150 natives working on the farm, but the pace was slow, the cost of jungle clearance being about £30 an acre. Baker paid his 'coolies' (the universal name for native labourers) 1 shilling a day, which was in fact the going rate for infantry soldiers back home. Clearly, rumours had reached the Bakers that their enterprise was regarded as the work of lunatics, so it was apt that the first fields to be sown were on Moon Plain. Elephants, oxen, horses and men worked to plant the oats with the help of Lord Ducie's culti- vator. The mid-century saw the rise of the 'golden age' of farming. At home, steam-driven threshing machinery began to replace the old methods, and a real practical science of soil husbandry was coming to the aid of farmers.

Baker was impressed with his elephant. She could do the work of three ox teams, and carried huge trunks for dam-building in her mouth. With only the lightest of handling by her mahout, she placed enormous timbers in exact positions. As we shall see in his hunting, Baker had enormous respect for a wild elephant too, referring to it, not the lion, as 'king of the beasts'.

The whole of the first year at Newera Ellia was dogged by misfortune. Wild hogs and 'elks' (sambur deer) constantly ravaged the oat fields, as did grubs. The Southdown ram died after eating too much clover, and the other two fought a duel to the death – by the following spring, only the Leicester ram remained. Twenty-six cattle died within days from an epidemic, and five Walers followed suit. 'Everything,' wrote Baker, 'seemed to be going into the next world as fast as possible.'[10]

Much grimmer was the loss of Mrs Fowler, the bailiff's wife. Popular and gentle, the woman had an unspecified recurring illness and died within the first year.

By trial and error, the Bakers coped. They realized that manure was essential, and used imported guano for the purpose. The soil was low on lime and magnesium. Potatoes, beans, peas, carrots and cabbages grew well, but not wheat.

In a reflective passage written in 1875, Baker commented on his original team. Hardly a man survived from it, but the Fowlers' pretty daughter had married, and one of the farmers returned to England with £300 in his pocket. The blacksmith married a 'good knock-about kind of a wife' whom Baker remembered using an 18-pound sledgehammer at her husband's forge. And Henry Perkes 'of elephant-jockeying notoriety' ended up as a successful groom, no doubt continuing to chat up the maidservants of Madras.

By the time Samuel left Ceylon in 1855, Newera Ellia had been tamed and was a prosperous estate. John continued to farm it, and Valentine obtained a commission in the green-jacketed Ceylon Rifles on his way to what everyone assumed would be a glittering military career, as befitted a brother of Samuel White Baker.

Chapter 4

Eight Years' Wandering

He may have been during his astonishing career an explorer, naturalist, governor, administrator and farmer, but what really motivated Samuel Baker was hunting. It dominated his leisure hours and was undoubtedly a factor in his choice of wanderings. Today, the wholesale destruction of wild animals is utterly unacceptable. Countries that continue to ignore such taboos, such as Japan with regard to whaling, are criticized in international conferences and become the target of wildlife activists. Individuals who still wear real fur coats are seen as murderers. We have become so obsessed with the fragility of planet Earth that we often forget the fact that it has been tumbling in space now for millions of years and will continue to do so long after we have gone. The end of species is a cyclical thing, no matter how it is achieved; if the dinosaurs had not disappeared, you might not be reading this today.

What is fascinating about Samuel Baker is that he began, like many of his contemporaries, with the excitement of the chase and came to realize, by the 1870s, that the *study* of wildlife was infinitely more rewarding than bringing down an elephant, gazelle or lion in the bush. To men of Baker's social class, hunting was a way of life. It was only misfits such as Oscar Wilde who could write of this group as 'the unspeakable in pursuit of the uneatable'; the county set revelled in it. Army regiments had their own hunts and many counties boasted two or three. The aristocratic elite, men who hit the headlines in the 1850s, like lords Cardigan and Lucan, owned their own packs of hounds (Wellington had taken one to Spain with him in 1808) and there was a huge social snobbery in jockeying for a place in, say, the Pytchley or the Quorn. Baker himself rode to hounds. Men (and women) of this class were expected to be excellent horsemen. Part of the opprobrium heaped on Robert Peel in the mid-1840s came not from the fact that he wanted to repeal the Tory Corn Laws, but that he was a bad rider; in the 1850s, while riding up Constitution Hill in London, his horse threw him and he died. Men in scarlet hunting across the muddy fields, the pack in full cry and the horns waking the misty morning is an abiding image of the English way of life which recent legislation has done little to destroy.

Baker was particularly interested in shooting. Shooting parties at weekend retreats became more popular as the century wore on. The aristocracy would invite anyone who was anyone for a four-day event beginning on a Friday and, with beaters and picnic baskets, blast away with obscenely expensive twelve-bore shotguns at anything that moved. For Baker, the grouse, partridge and deer set lacked that sense of excitement and danger he craved. He was most at home with a single bearer deep in the Sinhalese jungle or African bush, where his was the only gun and his quarry could, at any moment, turn and kill him.

He was still a teenager when he bought his first gun, a rifle he designed himself made by George Gibbs, a Bristol gunsmith. The weapon was huge. It weighed 21 pounds, had a 36-inch barrel and fired a ball of 3 ounces or a conical bullet of 4. It was a muzzle loader (breech loaders were not introduced until the 1850s) and it took a powerful man to fire it. The recoil was such that a weakling or novice might find themselves with a broken shoulder. In Britain only the largest Highland stags were large enough prey for a gun of this kind, but the weapon came into its own in wilder parts of the world. Baker also acquired a knife, broad-bladed and heavy, of the pattern made famous in America by Colonel James Bowie. Most of the studio photographs taken of Baker in the 1870s show him with this companion of a mile tucked into his belt. It was made by Paget of Piccadilly.

When Baker reached Ceylon, the animal he was least familiar with was the elephant. It was not until 1850 that a disbelieving public paid good money to see Britain's first, Jumbo, in London Zoo. So Baker went to the museum in Colombo and studied elephant skulls, and then he visited the live draught animals in the elephant compound and noted the exact position by which to bring such a beast down.

Hunting with his army friend Lieutenant de Montenac, he brought down elephants, deer and buffalo. This was not work for the women, and when his brothers joined him, he, John and occasionally Valentine set off for the interior as lightly equipped as possible. He 'started off with nothing but my guns, clothes, a box of biscuits and a few bottles of brandy – no bed, no pillow, no tent, nor chairs or table.' He had one gridiron and one saucepan, stewing or frying the game he caught. His hunting knife was his cutlery, a leaf was his plate and he drank from a coconut shell.

This boy's-own-adventure life suited Samuel Baker perfectly, and he was able to record the magic of it all years later:

> There cannot be a more beautiful sight than the view of sunrise from the summit of Pedrotallagalla ... which, rising to a height of 8,300 feet looks down on Newera Ellia, some 2,000 feet below ... There is a feeling approaching the sublime when a solitary man thus stands upon the highest point of earth [sic] before the dawn of day and waits for the first rising of the sun ... And now the distant hill-tops, far below, struggle through the snowy sheet of mist, like islands in a fairy sea.[1]

Not until the advent of television and cheap package holidays could most of us see sights like that.

It was on hunting expeditions like this that Baker the explorer began to develop. He realized that what to him were uncharted ravines, mountains and jungles were the natives' backyard. They had names for every plateau, stream and defile, and the jungle paths, though no more than deer runs, were actually centuries-old thoroughfares. And he discovered a series of water reservoirs or tanks, at Kardellai, Minneria and Padavelkellom, which were the archaeological remains and water supply of a once great medieval civilization: 'Well may Ceylon in those times have deserved the name of the "Paradise of the East".'[2]

What impressed Baker most were the ruins of Anaradupoora, a city of some 256 square miles; London was a village by comparison. His description of the wildlife he saw among these temples and walls was surpassed only by Rudyard Kipling in his Mowgli stories: 'The bear and the leopard crouch in the porches ... the owl roosts in the casements ... the jackal roams the ruins in vain.' His eyes were ever drawn to the man-made objects, and he was suddenly aware of the passing phase that was the age of man: 'There are gigantic idols before whom millions have bowed; there is the same vacant stare upon their features of rock which gazed upon the multitudes of yore; but they no longer stare upon the pomp of the glorious city, but upon rain and rank weeds and utter desolation.'[3] It was Kipling's 'letting in of the jungle', as Baker wrote: 'The population gone, the wind and the rain would howl through the deserted dwellings, the white ants would devour the supporting beams, the elephants would rub their colossal faces against the already tottering houses.'

In Ceylon, Baker came upon whole villages deserted by death. Cholera, dysentery and smallpox had contrived to wipe out whole populations – 'All dead; not one left to tell the miserable tale.' And he was aware of something that many 'greens' today have forgotten or never knew – the depredations of wildlife on human settlements. Dams were constantly being trampled down by the nomadic elephant herds which also ate their way through fields in a single night. Hogs rooted up crops, and birds pecked at the grain as the harvest ripened.

Forty years after he left Ceylon, Baker wrote *Wild Beasts and Their Ways,* another of his bestsellers avidly bought by a readership who were fascinated by such exotica. He divided the two-volume work into chapters on individual species, and devoted two of them to elephants. In his time, men pondered whether the elephant or the dog were more intelligent. Baker had no doubts – 'The Dog is man's companion; the Elephant is his slave.'[4]

Baker had ample opportunity to observe elephants in the wild and as game. Wild elephants shunned sunlight and ate at night, feeding wastefully in the sense of leaving whole branches uneaten, but they were very selective in their choice of tree. They had extraordinary powers of smell, picking up an enemy scent at 1,000 yards or more. Their trunks were particularly sensitive, despite the thick hide. Generally timid, elephants recoiled when threatened – Baker witnessed attacks by tigers on them and had a special armour made for one animal from sambur skin and buffalo hide. This made it totally impervious to claws or teeth. Baker was always pleasantly surprised by how sweet-smelling elephants were, largely because their digestion was rapid. On the march, in the more elaborate hunting trips, domestic elephants ate 800 pounds of green fodder, 1 pound of ghee (buffalo butter) with salt and jaggery (native sugar). Baker increased the daily ration of flour to 30 pounds per animal, making this into 'scones' weighing 2 pounds each and feeding them a little before sunset.

Ideally the elephants should bathe daily and be scrubbed all over by their mahout with a lump of brick or sandstone acting as a loofah. Elephants, Baker noted, were excellent swimmers, and a dead animal floated on its side, so high of the river surface that several men could ride on its flank like a raft. Domestic elephants were taught by fear, the ankus driven into their flanks, and Baker had some sympathy for them. Usually docile, when the beasts were in season (the 'must' period) they were unpredictable and moody. Even a casual slap of an elephant's trunk could do considerable damage. Like people, some were always friendly; others, to use Baker's phrase, were 'demented'.

The Indian species, with its smaller ears and inferior ivory, was generally smaller than the African, with shorter legs, so its speed was less. Baker was impressed by the animals' memories, knowing which plants were available at which seasons over huge areas of terrain. Today we are more familiar with the animals' feeding habits, mating and migratory patterns, and 'memory' is a human-ized way of looking at what are built-in traits. On the other hand, some of them did seem to have human habits. One elephant Baker had ridden recognized him again after a seven-month absence in England, although he admits that his feeding her sugar cane probably had a lot to do with it.

Baker writes of a rogue male from the Balaghat district of India's Central Provinces that killed its mahout and fled to the jungle. The beast roamed over a large area, attacking humans and tearing down houses and watch-places built to scare away scavengers. Rather than being frightened off by men's shouts, it was attracted to them and would suddenly loom out of the darkness on the edge of villages. Its method of killing was either to trample or pin a victim down with one foot and tear off heads and limbs with his trunk. His kill tally was twenty before a Colonel Bloomfield finally cornered him and put two bullets into his brain.

After a while in Ceylon, Baker had become a highly skilled hunter. He dressed in khaki[5] to blend with the countryside or green to lose himself in the jungle, and he had learned to move noiselessly, no easy task for a big man. He picked up animal spoor from disturbed water holes, broken twigs, flattened grass, bird alarm calls. He had nothing but contempt for the 'quiet, steady going people' at home who talked of 'unoffending elephants', 'poor buffaloes' and 'pretty deer'. To him, this was 'a variety of nonsense about things which they cannot possibly comprehend'. Such people, he noted, enthusiastically tucked into eels and lobster in England, not caring at all about how they are prepared (skinned alive in the case of the eel, boiled alive for lobsters).[6]

There was a government reward for the culling of wild elephants because of the damage they caused. It had been 10 shillings a tail, but this had dropped to 7, not because of any animalitarian change of heart on the government's part – they were simply having to pay out too much. In the 1840s a contemporary of Baker told of a hunt in which 104 elephants were shot by three hunters in three days. In those days, firearms were rare in Ceylon and the animals had no fear of them, standing around as the marksmen picked them off. Updating his book *Eight Years' Wandering in Ceylon* for a subsequent edition, Baker lamented the fact that so few elephant herds were left and blamed the natives, the Moormen in particular, for the wholesale slaughter.

Whole pages of the book deal with the calibre of guns, their range, rifling and so on, because a hard core of Baker's readers were would-be hunters with guns of their own, long before British law became obsessed with gun crime.[7] I will use just one example of an elephant hunt, although Baker gives no actual date for it. He and his friend Edward Palliser were tracking a bull along the banks of the Yallé river. Each man had two gun-bearers, Baker's carrying his four double No. 10 rifles, and he and Palliser carried single-barrelled guns for smaller game such as deer. As usual, the day began with a cup of hot chocolate (Baker did not like to hunt on a full stomach) and the four men followed the sluggish river until a chattering troupe of monkeys gave away the elephant's resting place. As the elephant was browsing on high branches with his head thrown back, Baker grabbed a No. 10 from his bearer and blasted the animal at an unusual angle through the jaw and up into his brain. A gun of that calibre was essential:

> The ball had to pass through the roots of the upper grinders and keep its course through hard bones and tough membranes for about two feet before it could reach the brain. This is the power which every elephant gun should possess; it should have an elephant's head under complete control in every attitude.[8]

A conical bullet might have glanced off.

While *Wild Beasts* concentrated on the tiger, the lion and bear, in Ceylon Baker was often hunting leopards. He distinguishes two species – the cheetah and the panther – but at the time, all spotted cats were called cheetahs by natives and white men alike. Leopards were hugely powerful animals, between 8 and 10 feet in length, capable of breaking a buffalo's neck with its fearsome leap. Baker knew that such big cats attacked first by stealth, inching forward through tall grass, then springing forward and sinking claws and teeth into its quarry's throat before twisting to snap the spine. Rips from the leopard's claws, though not instantly fatal, often caused gangrenous infection and a slow, lingering death.

One particularly ghastly example of the leopard's work stuck in Baker's mind. He was on his way back from a hunt, huddled on the saddle in the teeth of a torrential downpour, his dogs, bedraggled, splashing at his horse's heels. He rode past a Malabar boy, about 16 years old, squatting by the roadside in only a loincloth. Baker told him to go home or he would die of exposure in that weather. The boy said something, but did not move. Concerned when he got home, Baker sent runners back for the boy but he was already dead. Baker buried him and went back days later to pay his respects. The grave had been ripped up by leopards, which had left gnawed bones and funeral shrouds shredded on the ground.

Shooting leopards was particularly difficult because they were so hard to find, and Baker discusses in *Wild Beasts* the various types of trap that were used. The common variant was virtually a large mousetrap but far less effective – leopards had learned to be wary of them. Gun-traps were better, with a cocked weapon tied by string to the bait. The problem with this was that careless men could set this off with horrendous results. The traps that Baker set usually caught smaller animals, such as the civet cat – 'a very pretty and curious creature' – that fed on hares, chickens and rats. It was extensively trapped in Ceylon for the musk gland near its tail which was used by natives in their medicine. It could fetch, as a result, anything up to 6 shillings an animal.

Baker the budding naturalist could not resist commenting on other forms of Sinhalese wildlife. Muskrats were vermin in every sense, their vast numbers tainting human food because they urinated and defecated over it. Even wine could be spoiled in this way, because the corks became covered in the grim musk odour. Unknown in Britain, the bandicoot was particularly destructive, capable of eating a whole field of potatoes at one sitting. 'He is a perfect rat in appearance,' Baker wrote, 'but he would rather astonish one of our English tom-cats if encountered during his rambles.' He was most impressed by the ichneumon or mongoose that was so versatile at snake-killing that the natives left it alone. He himself never saw a mongoose–cobra duel, but he met many who had, and the mongoose 'never gives the contest until the snake is vanquished'.

One of the most dangerous animals that Baker hunted in Ceylon was the buffalo. On a hunt near Minneria Lake with his brother John, he came across a herd at the centre of which were seven large, bad-tempered bulls. It was mid-afternoon on a cloudless day and the Baker boys were carrying shotguns. Unfortunately, they had wandered far ahead of the bearers with the heavier weapons, and this almost proved fatal. A bull charged at them and both brothers fired simultaneously, shattering the beast's shoulder blade. As it veered off in pain, it was gored by another bull. While John finished off the wounded animal, Samuel went after the other one. Pinning it in a creek, Baker realized he had only two shots left. He blasted at the animal's chest, and although it was a clean hit, the bull had not moved. He fired again – his last shot – and still the animal stood there. Baker whistled loudly for John's help, then remembered the small change in his pocket to pay the 'coolies'. He poured the coins, with a double powder charge, down the barrel and waited for the bull to charge. John arrived at the crucial moment but his last shot did not bring the maddened animal down, and Samuel blasted away with the bull less than 2 feet from him. The brothers ran for it, now with no ammunition between them, and the bull staggered in a circle 'stunned by the collision with her Majesty's features upon the coin which he had dared to oppose'. The next morning, when the brothers returned expecting to find the bull dead, there was no sign of a carcase, and they never saw it again.

As Baker became more experienced as a hunter, he set out on expeditions better prepared. He took a light, waterproof tent, 15 feet in diameter and looking like a huge umbrella, which could sleep three but was light enough to be carried by bearers. A collapsible table fitted around the tent pole, and clothes, dressing table and gun rack completed the decor. He packed a dinner service for three in japanned tins and all the essentials for a life under canvas – a lantern, axe, bill-hook, matches, candles, a tinderbox, oil, tea, coffee, sugar, biscuits, brandy, wine, sauces, 'a few hams, meats and soups, a few bottles of curacao, a glass of which in the early dawn, after a cup of hot coffee and a biscuit, is a fine preparation for a day's work'.[9]

For more regular hunting expeditions, Baker built a hunting lodge – Elk Lodge – a few miles from Newera Ellia. It had a veranda, dining room, two bedrooms and an 8 foot fireplace, and was carpeted with deerskins. There was stabling for three horses, a kitchen, kennels and a shed which could house twenty 'coolies'. In one of his quieter moments, Baker wrote:

> Here, then, I am in my private sanctum [at Newera Ellia] my rifles all arranged in their respective stands above the chimney piece, the stags' horns round the walls hung with horn cases, powder flasks and the various weapons of the chase ... the thermometer is 62°F and it is midday. Even as I write the hounds are yelling in the kennel.

Baker's hunting clothes became refined as his time in Ceylon wore on. He wore a pair 'of tights, similar to ordinary elastic drawers, with a short jacket of the same material that fitted like a jersey. These were dyed green.' Photographs of him are striking because he is wearing short sleeves; most Victorian men simply wore their long

41

sleeves rolled. His ankle boots were relatively thin-soled and a broad leather belt held the ubiquitous knife.

Because of the huge distances involved, horses were essential on hunting trips, although they were tethered some distance from the quarry once the game was afoot. But like most huntsmen, Baker was particularly fond of his dogs. All over English country houses dating from the middle of the eighteenth century to the beginning of the twentieth there are portraits of the master and inevitably one or more faithful hounds. Baker had taken with him as part of his menagerie on the voyage to Ceylon foxhounds from the packs of the Duke of Beaufort and Lord Fitzhardinge, but discovered they were useless in the jungle. Apart from chasing everything that moved, they 'gave voice' as they had been trained on the English fox trail, and warned off game for miles around. Over the eight years in Ceylon, Baker bred his own dogs better suited to the country. They were crossbreeds, foxhounds mixed with pointers, bloodhounds and mastiffs, even Australian kangaroo hounds in various combinations. What he created were three types of dog used for different purposes. One tracked the scent – these were the finders. The second were the finders and seizers, a hybrid variety able to locate the quarry and hold it at bay. And third came the seizers, long-legged and powerfully jawed for the kill.

Baker was indeed fond of his dogs, and he genuinely grieved when they were killed or died of natural causes. His favourite seizers were Bran, Bertram, Killbrook, Hecate, Lucifer and Lora, all offspring of his original 'departed hero', Smut. Bertram was the bravest dog Baker had ever seen: 'He was a tall Manilla bloodhound with the strength of a lion,' always the first into the fray, 'but I prophesied an early grave for him, as no dog in the world could long escape death who rushed so recklessly upon his dangerous game.' Shortly after he wrote those words, Bertram was speared through the body by the horns of a buck elk and died.[10]

A single man could not conquer an area the size and complexity of Ceylon, but the restless Baker felt that, by 1855, the place had grown a little tame:

> The road encircles the plain and the carts are busy in removing the produce of the land. Here, where wild forests stood, are

gardens teeming with English flowers, rosy faced children and ruddy countrymen are about the cottage doors; equestrians of both sexes are galloping round the plains; and the cry of the hounds is ringing on the mountainside! And the church bell sounds where the elephant trumpeted of yore.[11]

It was time to move on for Samuel White Baker.

Chapter 5

Taking a Stroll

One of the favourite phrases that men remembered Samuel Baker using was to 'take a stroll'. This could mean a 20-mile trek through hostile jungle facing any number of dangers. The 'stroll' he took after leaving Ceylon, however, changed his life forever.

In 1855 he left Newera Ellia an ill man. Usually blessed with the constitution of an ox, a particular stroll to an unhealthy part of the island had laid him low with fever. One of his 'coolies' died of the same illness, as did his favourite horse, Jack. It was time for a break and he, Henrietta and the children set sail for home. 'The white cliffs of Old England rose hazily on the horizon,' he wrote at the end of *Eight Years' Wandering in Ceylon*, but he may already have realized that he no longer saw the place as his real home.

Henrietta was pregnant again and Baker's mother, Mary, had died in 1851, having not seen her sons for years. Samuel senior had remarried and bought an estate at Thorngrove in Worcestershire. Ever the family man, Samuel junior moved to Fladbury in the same county where his last child, Ethel, was born. In 1852 Baker had sent the manuscript of a book to Messrs Longman, the London publishers. It was called *The Rifle and Hound in Ceylon*, a mixture of sound practical advice on hunting techniques and exciting adventures. He sent his own sketches, which were redrafted by the publishers' in-house artist, and the book was a bestseller, being reprinted six times up to 1892.

So successful was this venture that Longmans demanded a sequel. This was *Eight Years' Wandering in Ceylon*, which I have quoted from extensively. This book, despite its criticisms of local imperial government, did even better and ran to seven editions by 1894. Baker finished the work at Fladbury and once it was done, he was off to Scotland, the wildest country he could find in Britain, to shoot stags with the Duke of Atholl. He was usually up at four in the morning, out with the beaters, learning the ways of red deer before liberal sensibilities were to close the season on them considerably.

On one occasion Baker convinced his host and his feisty head gamekeeper, Sandy MacCarra, to use the dogs in the way Baker had used them in Ceylon: in other words, track the deer, bring it to bay and let the dogs hold it until the shooters arrived to finish the animal off with a knife. MacCarra was opposed on the grounds that it would spoil the dogs and they would expect to tear any future kill apart too. Atholl gave him the go-ahead, however, and a huge party of onlookers, including the ladies, turned out to watch the result. A stag was found, and the hounds were allowed to bring it down before Baker killed it. MacCarra felt vindicated, but Baker wrote (in *Wild Beasts and Their Ways*), 'the venison did not belong to me, neither did the dogs', and smugly walked away.

On his return from Scotland, disaster struck. Henrietta was ill. She had loved the life at Newera Ellia, but it had been physically hard, and pregnancies and the loss of her babies had taken their toll. She missed Elizabeth, still in Ceylon, and could not readjust to the damp English climate. In the days before antibiotics and effective medicine, the 'cure' recommended by doctors to those clients who could afford it was to go abroad where a better climate could work wonders.

So the whole family – Samuel, Henrietta, their four daughters and Henrietta's sister Charlotte – all went to Bagnères-de-Bigorre in the Pyrenees. Here, while Henrietta recuperated, Baker could shoot bears. In this he was to be disappointed. The only beast that had been seen for months was shot by the local mayor, and Baker had to be content with eating the stew prepared from the animal. It was probably through gritted teeth that he declared it 'excellent'.

But far from providing a congenial climate, the Pyrenees killed Henrietta Baker, or, more precisely, typhus did. The endemic form of the disease, often called gaol fever in the nineteenth century, usually flared at times of overcrowding and deprivation. Napoleon's disastrous retreat from Moscow in 1812 saw thousands of men, already suffering from frostbite and exposure, succumb to it, and the high death rate in the potato famine of the 1840s had more recently given it the name 'Irish fever'. It was carried by fleas and ticks and could strike anywhere. For two weeks in the December of 1854, as Henrietta drifted in and out of consciousness, Baker hardly left her bedside. She died four days after Christmas, and the great white hunter was devastated.

Nothing of this comes through in Baker's writings. They are forceful, dominant and light-hearted, and reflect his usually cheerful disposition, but correspondence with his family reveals his sense of loss and desolation. He was suddenly a widower with four small children – the youngest still a baby – and he could not cope, perhaps for the only time in his life. Henrietta's sister Charlotte came to the rescue. She was only 22 but was typical of that stoical band of Victorian women – we find them as army wives and consorts of imperial civil servants – who rose to any occasion, and often did better than their men. She organized Henrietta's funeral and brought her brother-in-law and the girls back home.

Here the Baker family values kicked in, aunts and uncles visiting in droves to check that the girls were safe and happy. In a letter he wrote to John in March 1856, Samuel said:

> I have placed the children with Mrs Tapell [a governess] where they are comfortable, she being kindness itself. I took the dear little things down there with their good nurse Mary and I remained two days with them to make them feel at home. This they did immediately thank goodness and I left them quite happy; so soon do sorrows pass from their little minds.

The younger two could have no lasting memories of their mother at all, but Edith, the eldest, had, and she was a sickly child. 'You can imagine, my dear John, how terrible, how inconceivably miserable is my lot ... God grant that "time", that physician of all our woes, may bring some comfort, but I have no faith in it.'[1] There is no doubt that Samuel Baker was a loving father, but the hands-on bringing up of four girls was probably beyond his capabilities. For men like him, the answer to heartbreak was to travel, 'to stroll', to immerse himself in action. And there was a war on.

By the time Baker decided to sail for the Crimea at the end of 1855 – the journey took two weeks by steamer and could cost as little as £5 – the war was, in fact, nearly over, but his brothers Valentine and James were both out there, in the 12th Lancers and 8th Hussars respectively, so it made some sense. The extraordinary gallantry of the army had shown itself in the autumn with the battles of the Alma and Balaclava. The 8th Hussars had taken part in the suicidal Charge of the Light Brigade, but James Baker had not been with them then; by the merest chance he was riding in the escort to Lord Raglan on the Sapouné Heights above the battlefield. The army had settled down in its windblown camp on the heights above Balaclava as the winter all but destroyed it, and at home men such as John Roebuck launched an official investigation into the war's mishandling. Lord Raglan, the 71-year-old commander-in-chief, died in the Crimea, to be replaced by younger, abler men, and the French, Britain's new-found ally, were left to take the Allies' objective, the seaport of Sebastopol.

The spring had seen better weather, the building of a railway and Mary Seacole's famous hotel for officers. Reinforcements, including new regiments such as the 12th Lancers with Valentine Baker, arrived with the snow's thaw; the rest was merely a mopping-up operation. Samuel Baker intended to join the Turkish contingent. He held no queen's commission of course, but all wars in this period were characterized by noble amateurs. Officers in the cavalry and infantry bought their commissions, and of the 2,000 plus officers who served in the Crimea, less than 5 per cent had attended the training school at Sandhurst. It was also the era of the 'TG' – the travelling gentleman – who went out to watch the action and took a picnic hamper with him. The Germans called such men *Schlachtenbumlers*, battle walkers. One look at the Turkish contingent, however, probably made Baker change his mind. It had eight cavalry regiments and sixteen infantry and six artillery units; its officers were European and the men Turkish. Unfortunately, the Turks had a poor reputation among the British. They had no uniform or discipline, and were all tarred with the same brush of brutal incompetence as the Bashi-Bazouks, light cavalry who were virtually bandits on horseback. Baker could see at once that this was 'a sort of refuge for the destitute', and he considered operating as a freelance agent for the government, touring as a private citizen through the Circassian mountains to 'judge of the facilities for a Russian attack upon India'. For the rest of the century, Britain's biggest fear in Europe was Russia. The foreign policy of every government from now on assumed that the Russian plan was to expand southwards, pressing Turkey again (as happened in 1877) or directly threatening British India (as in 1878).

In the event, nothing materialized for Baker's restless spirit. He dined at the 12th Lancers' mess with Valentine across the Bosphorus at Scutari, made famous by Florence Nightingale as her base hospital, and went with him and a friend to Sabanja on the shores of the Sea of Marmara where they hunted red deer, duck, wolves and bears. Valentine and James were sharing a house on the Bosphorus with William Tottenham, colonel of the 12th Lancers, and it was here that Valentine began the first of his important books on cavalry tactics.

By the time Baker returned to England, brother John and his family had come home from Ceylon and had settled to a life of fox-hunting in the Warwickshire countryside around Rugby. At this period – and it is a measure of how lost he was – Baker toyed with a career in the Church. Clearly the loss of Henrietta had made him turn to the spiritual, but in the end he pursued it no further. His biographer Richard Hall sees in the jerky, disordered handwriting of the letter he wrote discussing this to a friend all the signs of an imminent nervous breakdown and this may be so. He was 35, active, able and intelligent, and had enough money, had he chosen, to do nothing for the rest of his life; but that was not the Baker way.

The autumn of 1857 found him hunting in Scotland again, and it was here he met the extraordinary Punjabi exile Duleep Singh, hunter, playboy and maharajah, with a government pension of £50,000 a year. Duleep Singh is an odd character, at once appallingly rich and spoilt, and yet a prisoner, exiled by the British from his own land. The East India Company's incursions into his native Punjab in the early 1840s had brought a head-on clash with the most for-midable opponents in India – the Sikhs. With a warrior tradition and formidable artillery, and having been trained in European war-fare by the French in the eighteenth century, the Sikhs were ruled until 1839 by Ranjit Singh, the Lion of the Punjab, who was Duleep's father. The wily old maharajah was, like other members of his family, murderous and ambitious, but he was sensible enough to leave the British alone. His successors were not. They fought each other for his inheritance and the fabulous diamond called the Koh-i-noor, and effectively let the British in by crossing the River Sutlej, thereby breaking the Treaty of Lahore of 1826.

Two wars later the Sikh state was beaten and the British army added Aliwal, Chilianwallah and a half-dozen others to its battle honours. As it happened, the Sikhs afterwards remained largely loyal to the Raj, but in case any nationalist cause should be revived, the heir to the Punjab, the 11-year-old Duleep, was effectively placed under house arrest by the British and was moved to different locations in India. Here he was kept apart from other Sikhs, converted to Christianity and counted two English boys as his best friends.

In 1854 the maharajah, still only 16, was brought to England. His charm and vivacity captivated Victoria and Albert, and while a guest at Osborne in the Isle of Wight he was painted in all his magnificence by Winterhalter, the court artist. He was a strikingly handsome young man, his turban bejewelled and swirling over his waist-length black hair, the ends of which were tied, Sikh fashion, under his chin. The queen wrote in her journal: 'He is certainly very attractive. Extremely high-principled and truthful, with most gentlemanlike and chivalrous feelings, but rather indolent and not caring to learn or read; this, due probably to his Indian nature.'[2]

Victoria was probably a little unsure of the maharajah striking up a friendship with her own son Bertie – the future Edward VII – three years Duleep's junior. She was all too aware of Bertie's indolence. Duleep won the hearts of all he met, and to imperialists made a perfect case for all that was good about the British empire. The maharajah spoke excellent English, played cricket and when in Scotland wore Highland dress. Above all, he had brought with him the Koh-i-noor, which he presented to a delighted Queen Victoria, and which became a central part of the crown jewels. Technically, the jewel was acquired by Lord Dalhousie, the governor-general of India, and it had to be cut down to fit the state crown.

Duleep Singh was given large houses in Wimbledon and Roehampton, and accompanied his mentors Lord and Lady Login on a grand tour of Europe in 1854–55. On his return, he leased Castle Menzies in Perthshire, and by 1858 had added the Earl of Breadalbane's magnificent house at Auchlyne. He was 19 when he met

Samuel Baker that year, and the two became instant kindred spirits. Oddly, Duleep does not feature in Dorothy Middleton's biography of Baker, but as it turned out the flashy maharajah was to be instrumental in a change of direction for the white hunter. The two planned a shooting expedition to the plains of Hungary from November 1858 to March 1859. This was partly because of the dearth of decent game in Scotland. *The Field*, a sporting magazine for which Baker occasionally wrote, noted that some sportsmen, vowing not to return to the Highlands for two or three seasons until the numbers had increased, went to Norway or Germany in search of sport. (This situation would find no resonating chord today – it was precisely the over-shooting of game that made it scarce. Between them, on one grouse shoot, Baker and the Liberal MP William Price had bagged 355 birds and 91 rabbits and hares.)

There were those who raised eyebrows – and voices – of concern over the Hungarian expedition. For all Britain's success in the Crimea and her prompt putting down of the mutiny in India by the end of 1857, central Europe was not in Britain's remit, and it was a dangerous place. The revolutions which had broken out all over Europe in 1848 had seriously rocked the Austro-Hungarian empire, and violence had broken out at Budapest in March of that year. With hindsight, of course, the revolutions were largely middle-class and intellectual, demanding constitutions and rights on the British model, and probably both Baker and Duleep could feel a little smug about that. The reality, however, was that the old kingdoms and principalities were collapsing in all directions, and refugees flooded out of the area, scattering everywhere and often at odds with the group who had settled next door. Whole villages were destroyed in Hungary as first bandits, then the army, then the idealists, then the army again, tried to assert their authority. 'Who can judge,' asked Edward Bauernfeld in 1848, 'how far a wildly excited and un-educated mob can be led by the Utopia of the abolition of property, of the common ownership of goods? In short, anarchy stood clearly before my eyes.'[3] By September 1849, when the Russian army had been brought in to put down the Hungarian rising, the Magyar poet Sandor Petöfi wrote: 'You Serbs, Croats, Germans, Slovaks, Romanians, / Why do you all ravage the Hungarian? / There shall be no peace until the last drop of blood / Flows from your evil

51

hearts.'[4] The Austrian poet Franz Grillparzer saw the futility of it all – 'From humanity via nationalism to inhumanity'[5] – and George Trevelyan, the great British historian wrote – '1848 was the turning point at which modern history failed to turn.'[6]

Despite objections, the Hungarian expedition went ahead. The area chosen was awash with wild boar, bear and wildfowl, and money was no object to either Baker or Duleep Singh. The plan was to travel by train to Vienna, then by steamer down the Danube, ending up, via Greece, in Rome, where the maharajah intended to meet up with Bertie, the Prince of Wales, who was undergoing his own 'grand tour' in a desperate attempt by his father to turn him into a cultivated clone of himself. In Rome, Lady Login would be waiting with an Indian princess to whom she was chaperone, who might be a suitable wife for the maharajah in an age of arranged titled marriages.

At the end of November, Baker wrote a hurried letter to Edith, his eldest daughter, now 10, reminding the girls that they should wash only in hot water, as 'lukewarm water is horrid', and he was sorry to have missed them.

Unbeknownst to Baker, the queen was having last-minute reservations about the trip. The *Illustrated News of the World* pulled no punches with the text accompanying the lithograph of Duleep Singh. His mother, 'the Messalina[7] of the Punjab', had the 'lowest and most profligate habits'; his father was the epitome of 'low excesses and debauchery'. Lady Login, ever the maharajah's moral guardian, wrote to Victoria wondering whether Baker was of sufficient probity to accompany the young, naive and giggling prince. He was an 'habitué of eastern cities', which is more likely to refer to the fleshpots of Istanbul than the backwaters of Colombo. But Duleep Singh was adamant – it was Baker or no one.

At Ostend, wearing English tweeds and with his hair cut short, the maharajah claimed to be Captain Robert Melville,[8] and the pair travelled on across the Rhineland. For Baker, it may have been a little nostalgic – after all, he had spent time in Frankfurt, leaving the boring ways of business and getting in all the shooting he could. Their first port of call was Hanover, not yet annexed by Prussia in its drive to German unification, but conversely no longer belonging to Britain; its current ruler, George V, was blind, and determined after the revolutions of 1848 to put the clock back in terms of democracy. At Magdeburg they found a thriving port on the Elbe that was the capital of Westphalia, and had been all but flattened in the Thirty Years' War. Berlin on the Spree was the capital of the increasingly pushy Prussia, and when Baker passed through had a population of half a million, with broad, gas-lit boulevards courtesy of Frederick the Great in the previous century. Breslau was small by comparison, with a rich and often-occupied past, and fast on its way to becoming a railway centre.

At Vienna, the beautiful heart of the Austrian empire, the newspaper *Wiener Zeitung* listed the travellers in their 'new arrivals' column. 'Samuel Baker, rentier in London; Robert Melville, ditto'. The term 'rentier' was universal European shorthand for man of leisure. Here the pair saw little sign of the revolution that had overthrown Prince Metternich ten years earlier. The Habsburgs were still very much in power. Duleep Singh now appeared in his Indian finery and was presented to the side-whiskered Emperor Franz Josef; the latter would not quite live to see the destruction of his empire on the barbed wire of the First World War. Duleep and Baker hunted boar with Duke Esterhazy and discussed the finer points of taxidermy, then at the height of its popularity. The expedition was monitored by the British papers, the *Daily News* recording the pair's next phase of the journey.

In the winter they reached Budapest, where they visited a resident English architect, Adam Clark, who had been building a bridge linking Buda and Pest for ten years, only to see it knocked down time and again by marauding armies. Buda was 'the Paris of the East', and the maharajah and his companion lost no time in visiting operas, theatres and cafés where wild gypsy music played until dawn.

It was in Pest that Duleep picked up a 'wife', as the papers reported it. On 16 January 1859 the Vienna *Freuden-Blatt* wrote: 'The Maharajah Duleep Singh, well known in English fashionable circles, has chosen unto himself a bride at Pest. They are now resting at Semlin. The marriage will take place at Galantz and after the ceremony the young couple will proceed to India.' The *Frachshofer Journal* took up the tale, and when Victoria read it in the British papers three days later, she must have thought Lady Login's warnings about Baker fully justified. There was little doubt that the maharajah *had* picked up a girl, and spent Christmas and the New Year with her at Semlin as the papers reported. It is possible that the 'Black Prince' was a virgin and that the lady was in fact a high-class courtesan who made a man of him, rather as an Irish prostitute was said to have seduced the Prince of Wales around this time. Baker wrote later to the Duchess of Atholl that there was not the 'slightest foundation' in rumours of marriage to a 'Wallachian [Romanian] lady of high rank'.[9] It was what Baker did *not* say that would probably give us the truth.

The Danube was a treacherous river. Steamers could not navigate the entire length, but neither Baker nor Duleep lost much sleep over that. They hired a 70-foot covered boat and oarsmen to go with it, and set off, complete with three stoves, wood, beer, wine and champagne. While Baker could have coped perfectly well by himself, the maharajah always travelled in style, accompanied by three English servants and a whole arsenal of hunting rifles. They shot the rapids known as the Iron Gates, but near Vidin the boat was holed by ice and the pair put up in fairly atrocious local accommodation, paying their respects to the local pasha, as was the custom when titled (albeit powerless) potentates came calling. The hunting had been a disappointment to Baker. The maharajah was 'as I expected, of too soft a texture for the successful pursuit of large game in midwinter in a wild country'. Few people, after all, had Baker's strength, speed and tenacity, able to run over the purple heather or the scraping scrub at the pace of the hounds.

At Vidin the revolutionary Louis Kossuth had first holed up after the failure of 1848, and the Russians and Austrians had consuls in the town. The place was rough, with gangs of Albanian soldiers carousing into the small hours. They eyed Baker and the maharajah with suspicion. What were a white man and a black companion, who had a white girl with him, doing in their town in the middle of winter? And if they were spies, who were they working for? It was in this volatile country, where settlements had gone, men had died and no one felt safe, that the travelling Englishman and Punjabi visited a slave auction.

And one of the winning bidders that day was Samuel White Baker.

Chapter 6

'Flooey'

'The second Mrs Baker,' wrote Samuel years later, 'was not a screamer,' and that was just as well, bearing in mind what she experienced both before and after she met the Ceylon sportsman.

In the 1850s the world focus of slavery lay in the United States. The 'peculiar institution', as the *New York Times* described it in 1854, was dividing the American house against itself. Legislation was brought in relating to fugitive slaves, black runaways who fled their southern plantations in search of freedom. A powerful abolitionist lobby with effective champions such as William Lloyd Garrison challenged the white supremacists who ran those plantations, and the mindless 'white trash' who would as soon shoot a black man as a dog. And the rhetoric was turning to violence. In 1859, the year that Baker met his future wife, the abolitionist John Brown of Ossowatomie wrote, 'I ... am now quite certain that the crimes of this guilty land will never be purged away, but with Blood' – his subsequent raid on the arsenal at Harper's Ferry and his own hanging were the result. And that in turn presaged civil war.

Slavery in the East was a different matter. In the Ottoman empire, decaying and decadent, it had a long history. As the Turks swept north-west in the late Middle Ages, conquering Christian state after Christian state, they forced the vanquished to pay the *devşirme*, the boy tribute, in which children as young as 5 were sold to the sultan to provide janissaries (mercenaries) for his army or eunuchs for his harem. Nicolas de Nicolay was horrified in 1551 when he saw a slave market in Tripoli, North Africa:

> I went to see the Turks' market, which they call a bazaar and which is where the poor Christians captured in Sicily, Malta and Gozo are sold to the highest bidders. In accordance with

ancient oriental custom, slave dealers are allowed to parade their captives quite naked to show that they have no physical defects and to have their eyes and teeth inspected as if they were horses.[1]

The method by which Baker acquired his wife was odd, and to middle- and upper-class Victorians not at all acceptable. As late as 1949, Baker's biographer Dorothy Middleton does not mention the auction at all. Baker himself never wrote of it, and his family were anxious to accept his new wife because she had clearly been responsible for bringing Samuel back from his own personal abyss.

Underlying Samuel's life – and that of Valentine, as we shall see – is a dark, rather disturbing thread of sexuality, made to seem all the more disturbing against middle-class society's dread of such topics. Sex was taboo. It clearly happened, but behind closed doors, and there must be no overt reference to it. Euphemisms abounded in polite society – underwear became 'necessaries'; legs were 'nether limbs'; breasts were 'baby's public house'. Middle-class men expected to marry virgins, whatever their own sexual experience, and marital sex was for procreation. Anything more adventurous usually involved courtesans who knew their business. Men in Baker's circle were notorious for this; today, Edward, Prince of Wales – 'Bertie' – would probably be discreetly admitting himself for therapy as a 'sexaholic'. Richard Burton, Baker's fellow African explorer, was renowned for his string of mistresses, of all nationalities and hues. Another explorer, John Speke, fathered at least one child by an African, and his publisher had to eliminate all references to it in Speke's books. On the Hungarian trip, as we have seen, Duleep Singh was involved with probably a high-class call girl.

So, as Richard Hall puts it, 'We cannot tell whether Sam Baker was moved by pity or desire.'[2] Perhaps it was both. Florenz Barbara Maria Finjanjian Sazasz was a striking-looking blonde, aged at most 17, and caught Baker's eye on the platform at Vidin. Slave auctions for harem girls were sophisticated affairs. The auction room was the *selamlik*, the men's room, hung with expensive tapestries and lit by chandeliers. The bidders would lounge on the divans, drinking coffee and eating sweetmeats while they made their selections. Girls such as Florenz were never exhibited naked, and came with certifications of virginity. She twirled on the equivalent of the cat-walk, while a eunuch read out her attributes. She was from Hungary and spoke two languages, as well as being an excellent dancer and horsewoman. She had been trained for this moment for ten years.

Florenz's most recent biographer, Pat Shipman, is in no doubt that there was a flash of sympathy between Baker and the girl, and she also believes that Florenz had no idea of the ramifications of the slave auction until she was actually up for sale. She was vulnerable, not that much older than Baker's oldest daughter, and had possibly been in a highly dangerous and inhospitable situation. Samuel Baker was not technically a public schoolboy, but he behaved like one that day and tried to outbid everyone else. One version of the story, which Ms Shipman accepts, is that he was outbid by the agent of the local pasha, who wanted Florenz for himself, and that Baker bribed an official to smuggle the girl into his carriage with Duleep. If this is true, the traveller had managed to offend two civilizations at once – the British, because he had obtained a slave, and the Ottoman because he had broken the rules of the harem auction. Subsequently, he did not give Florenz her freedom (according to Turkish law she was his property) but kept her with him.

So bizarre was his decision that elements in British society would never understand it, much less accept it. It was one thing to support the Turks militarily – as in the Crimean War – but that was merely to give the Russian bear a bloody nose. It was another thing entirely to take part in a slave auction, which looked suspiciously like con-doning the practice. And until 1833 of course, the Bakers had been slave-owners themselves. Polite society at home would have shud-dered. White slavery was topical: the *Morning Post* in 1857 wrote that there was 'an absolute glut in the Turkish market of white, human flesh'. Most of the slaves were female, either from Georgia or the Caucasus, and the going rate was anything above £5. The highest recorded price in today's terms was £21,000. The favourite ages were between 12 and 18, and the upheaval of the 1850s in the Balkans had added considerably to their numbers.

Florenz's past is shrouded in mystery and she kept it that way, either because it added to a sense of excitement for all who met her or because it was genuinely too painful to recount. Her highborn name seems to have been genuine, and although she eventually spoke a number of languages fluently, her German/Hungarian accent remained strong all her life. There was talk of her witnessing the murder of her family in the bloody chaos that followed 1848. On the other hand there was talk that she had been a concubine in the local pasha's harem (such girls were schooled in the art of lovemaking from as young as 12), and that she was a parting gift from the pasha to Baker as he continued his Danube journey. She was also, according to some, the illegitimate daughter of the Emperor Franz Josef, although he was only eleven years her senior, and her mother was an aristocrat living on the Hungarian border; the girl had been swept off her feet by Baker on a shooting trip.

The most reliable version is Robin Baily's account.[3] Baily was Baker's nephew and would serve under him in the Sudan years later. His aunt Beatrice, Samuel's sister-in-law, became Florence's close friend (Baker used the Anglicized form of her name almost immediately), and the violence of the woman's early years and the slave auction story comes from this source. Florence had been doing her best to survive with her family, their property and cash gone, and with only her old nurse for companionship. The woman's death in 1859 brought the girl as a slave to Vidin, and the rest was history.

If the story of Baker's effective abduction of Florence is true, this would certainly explain the hasty abandonment of the hunting expedition and the dash across country. Baker and Duleep Singh hired three coaches and rattled for 200 miles across southern Romania for Bucharest. 'We were five days jolting at full gallop over a wild country of frozen deep ruts without the semblance of a road,' Baker wrote. 'Your backbone nearly sticks into the cushion.'[4]

It was at Bucharest that Baker and Duleep Singh parted company. The maharajah had had a whale of a time, but he enjoyed his comforts too much to rough it Baker-style, and by 11 February he was in a soft bed in the Hotel d'Angleterre in Constantinople, too exhausted to accept many invitations to soirees. When Lady Login met up with him as planned in Rome, she wrote in her diary, with a great deal of smugness no doubt, that the whole thing 'had been rather a fiasco', and that Baker had not, as she had prophesied, been 'a wise counsellor to a young and inexperienced charge'. The counsel might have worked in an indirect way – when Duleep Singh married, his wife was a child, the daughter of a slave, from an American mission school on the Nile.

In Bucharest, Baker had time to draw breath. He and Florence stayed, in separate rooms, at the Manuk Hotel. His 'bride' (the couple were not in any sense actually married) spoke no English as yet, and whereas few people in Romania asked any questions of the rugged Englishman, a return to England with her was out of the question. Over the months that followed, while she learned his language with astonishing speed, he tried to piece together her past. As a small child she remembered 'shots, knives, yells, corpses and fire' – almost certainly the attack on her family in the year of revolutions. She was born, she told him, in Transylvania, the 'land beyond the forest' in the Carpathians, a dark place haunted by tales of vampires, were-wolves and the lasting reputation of its long-dead ruler, Vlad Dracula, the Impaler. Since Florenz had a German name, she was probably descended from the 'Saxons', middle-class merchants who settled in Transylvania from the fourteenth century. She was born on 6 August 1841 and was a Catholic. The name 'Finjanjian' that she occasionally used came from the Armenian family who looked after her following her parents' probable murder.

'Looked after' was something of a euphemism. Florence's father, Madteos, had been the adjutant to General Bem, a nationalist soldier fighting for Hungarian independence under Louis Kossuth in 1848. When a joint Austro-Russian army defeated Bem, Florence's family fled south to Vidin in the Ottoman empire, hopefully beyond the reach of the vengeful authorities, who were out for blood. The existence of these refugees caused problems for the sultan, as by law he should have handed them back to Austria. In the chaos that fol-lowed, with some men accepting Islam in order to stay and others, promised amnesty, returning home, both of Florence's parents disappeared. She was taken to Finjanjian Hanim, the woman who handled slave auctions in Vidin. It was now that Barbara Maria became Florenz – 'flower' in Armenian.

How soon Florenz and Samuel became lovers is unknown. Pat Shipman pictures Baker behaving as a perfect gentleman and waiting for her to make the first move. Richard Hall believes that Baker's first marriage to Henrietta was 'respectably humdrum' in that he does not refer to her at all in his Ceylon books. (This hardly

squares with the devastation he felt over her death. The books that
Baker wrote were 'boy's own adventures' that still have an appeal
today. They were not read by women and were not written for
them.) The couple spoke in German (Baker's clearly quite rusty by
this time). He knew he could not let her go. They may have exchanged vows – Baker told his friend Stuart-Wortley this was the
case – but that carried no weight in the eyes of the Church or the
law.

One way to avoid parting – 'Flooey' quickly became very important to Samuel Baker – was to find something to do in Romania and
the opportunity presented itself, as it so often did to Victorian
gentlemen, via the old-boy network. It was all about railways. The
first Romanian to ride a train was probably Petrache Poenaru, a
student who found himself on the Liverpool to Manchester line in
October 1831: 'I travelled by a new means of transport, which
represents one of the miracles of the industry of this century ...
twenty carriages bound together, loaded with 240 people are
dragged by only one steam machine.'[5] The railway arrived only
slowly in eastern Europe. While railway mania saw the building of
thousands of miles of track in Britain, it was not until August 1854
that the first Romanian line, designed to carry coal for 60 miles, was
opened.

It was the British who were the railway builders, and a British
company was now in business setting up a line from Bucharest to
Constanza on the Black Sea, as an obvious outlet to the port. One of
the company's directors was William Price, the MP Baker had shot
grouse with six years earlier. Baker pulled strings, talked to Charles
Liddell, the Danube and Black Sea Company's chief engineer, and
got himself an administrative post. In the three weeks he waited for
confirmation, Baker wrote home to his sister Min (Mary) and to his
eldest daughter. He told them all about Bucharest and his new
position, but it would be seven years before he told them about
Florence.

The post he was taking on sounded so unlike the adventurous
Baker that he built up its importance. He wrote in March 1859 to his
friend Stuart-Wortley: 'I have now accepted the post as General-
Manager of the Company ... I shall be obliged to remain here for

two years, after which I shall return to England.' In the meantime, despite grandiose ideas of silver and china he would import for the manager's residence, the area provided all the hardships he was used to; fleas were as big as bantam cocks and bugs as large as turbots; the streets of Bucharest were filthy, 5 inches deep in mud.

Baker toyed with a government post emerging from all this. All over Europe there were consuls, ambassadors, residents, 'our men in ...', and in view of his later career, this made perfect sense. He visited Robert Colquhoun, the British consul in Bucharest, who was another old shooting acquaintance from Scotland, and put his case. It seems likely that Colquhoun disapproved of Baker's acquisition of Florence; certainly he pulled no strings on Baker's behalf.

Having accepted the railway job, the 'Bakers' went to Constanza. The town was not impressive but the navvies laying track smashed their way through the old Roman fortifications, built by Trajan when he conquered what was then Dacia in the second century, and Baker was delighted, with his schoolboy passion for such things, to find ancient bath houses, marble columns and coins. The job was not his métier – he had detested office work when a clerk for his father in London – but with typical Baker resolve he threw himself into it enthusiastically. 'My staff will soon be organized,' he wrote to Min in April. 'My office is being built as fast as possible; and I am daily expecting the arrival of book-keepers and clerks. Imagine my being anxious for the completion of the Office! I hear you say "Samuel also among the Prophets!" or, in modern phraseology "Sam among the clerks".'[6] And of course he found time to shoot, and take the dogs out on the Black Sea marshes. The flats teemed with wild geese and the Danube was alive with fish.

The new man was not popular with the Barklay family, four sons of an East Anglian vicar who were in charge of the railway construction. If they resented the nepotism that had got Baker the job as their boss, that was hypocrisy at its best. Only Jack, the eldest, had an engineering bent – and that was self-taught. George, Robert and Henry were there because they were Barklays. Henry wrote home, 'We are expecting a Mr Baker, the great elephant shooter, as managing director ... If he is a nice man he will be a great addition to our party.'[7] It was true that Baker knew nothing about railways, and his obsession with shooting and fishing quickly grated. Henry wrote that he had just returned from a trip, finding Jack in a solitary state 'as he is not fond of having much to do with *The Bakers'* (Barklay's emphasis). When Henry Barklay wrote two books of reminiscences about his time in Romania he never mentioned the Bakers at all, even though by then they were world famous.

In December 1859 a severe storm in the Black Sea saw a ship washed up on the Constanza shore. While others watched helpless from the quayside, Baker saw a survivor clinging to a shattered spar and leapt in to rescue him. For a man who had waded through icy Scottish rivers this was no great feat, and he dragged the man to safety.

The new-found relationship between 'Mr and Mrs Baker' – he almost certainly introduced her as his wife in Constanza – may be recorded obliquely in the novel that Baker subsequently wrote, *Cast up by the Sea*, and the heroine Polly is probably Florence. In one scene the husband, Paul, 'tenderly wiped the tears from her large blue eyes and warmly kissed her forehead'. And there is little doubt that it was Florence and not Henrietta who was the real love of his life.

Baker wrote fourteen articles for *The Field* in this period, full of vivacity and humour, under the pen-name Phantom. He wrote about duck-shooting in the mud, comparing the vast armies of frogs with people – 'assuming and bumptious'. He wrote about bird migration patterns and the social life in Romania. Bucharest was riddled with gambling dens, and the landowning class was debauched. By contrast the ordinary people were quiet, well-behaved and clean. He was grimly moved by Tartar refugees who landed at Constanza, driven out of their homelands by the aggression of the Russians. Nor was life in Constanza all that safe. In the Turkish-run town, brigands were shot and their heads impaled on spikes in the market square. 'Indolence, cruelty, avarice and sensuality,' wrote Baker, 'have succeeded in rendering comparatively barren the fairest and richest land in Europe.' In some ways, the great elephant shooter, the overgrown schoolboy, was growing up.[8]

In May 1860 Baker went home. He left Florence in Constanza, probably still unable to introduce her in England in any way that would be acceptable. He was officially winding up his contract with the Danube and Black Sea Railway Company and entering the next and most dazzling phase of his life. He was back by June, and Henry Barklay wrote: 'Baker has come out but nobody of our party has seen him and as he is *nobody* now we don't want to.'[9] I doubt whether Samuel Baker would have noticed this pettiness. He and Florence moved out of the manager's house overlooking the harbour and lived for a while with Tartar refugees. He spent the time hunting wolves along his ex-company's track.

In October, Baker sold the cargo ship he had used to ferry supplies and did not attend the lavish opening of the railway line. The project had cost £500,000 and was historic in that it was the first true railway line to be opened in Romania. The couple took a steamer from Constanza through the Sea of Marmara to Scutari, where Valentine had served with the 12th Lancers and shared the house with brother James.

Baker was still contributing to *The Field*, and in one telling article he described the idea of owning a harem: 'surrounded by a multiplicity of beauties – dark eyes and blue, black hair and every shade towards gold ... ravishing forms that we read about in eastern novels. Five and twenty wives going out shopping and you pay the bills! Can any man of feeling conceive anything more horrible?'[10]

No doubt, gentlemen at home reading this over their morning coffee would have chuckled and agreed, but there was a darker, even smuttier side to all this. 'Eastern novels' were the pornography of their day – like *The Lustful Turk* (1827), which deals with the horrors of a white girl drawn into the clutches of the insatiable dey. Baker even hints at his own predilections – 'being by nature wicked, I very improperly watched their selections' – when he observed a harem's purchases being carried by their eunuchs from his hotel window, which seems harmless enough. But when one of the wives chose a crinoline, 'I had an intense longing to see her try it on.' So, no doubt, did his gentlemen readers!

Constantinople was a vast, sprawling mess. Drunken sailors roamed the streets, stall-holders harangued passers-by, selling leather goods, 'sweetmeats' ('Turkish delight') and jewellery. From there, Baker and Florence went on what was essentially a honeymoon. They took the steamer for the ten-hour trip to Izmit, and then went by horseback to Sapanga, where they rented part of a private house. On the floor below was a cowshed, so milk was handy. It snowed and Baker plunged through the drifts hunting boar. He was usually alone, but on Friday – the Muslim holy day – he was joined by dozens of locals, all anxious to shoot with the great hunter, Samuel White Baker.

Chapter 7

Into the Dark Continent

In a letter to one of his family, Samuel Baker wrote in December 1860, 'You know that Africa has always been in my head.' He wrote to his sister Min to explain why he was not coming home: 'A wandering spirit is in my marrow which forbids rest. The time may come when I shall delight in cities; but at present I abhor them. My magnetic needle directs me to Central Africa.'[1]

Baker's fellow explorer Richard Burton famously wrote, 'Madness comes from Africa,' but he did not write that until 1881, twenty years after both of them were searching for the sources of the Nile. In 1860 the interior of Africa was indeed the 'dark continent'. The far north from Egypt to Morocco had a very long history of international commerce, and Europeans knew it well. Egypt in particular pulled the intellectuals of all western countries because of its impressive ruins and the almost embarrassing amount of its archaeology. The far south too, having been explored first by the Portuguese, was home to the Dutch Boers, who lived uneasily alongside the Zulu on the one hand and the British on the other. There were European trading posts and mission stations along the coast, east and west, but the heart of Africa remained unmapped and a source of fascination. The Spanish conquistadors of the sixteenth century had gone to the New World in the Americas with 'Gold, God and Glory' emblazoned on their banners, and these three inducements remained in place for Africa in the second half of the nineteenth century.

There were legends in Africa that men found fascinating. Somewhere – and writers such as Rider Haggard cashed in on it – lay the fabulous mines of the biblical King Solomon. Somewhere 'beyond the mountains of the moon' was the kingdom of the Christian king Prester John (which John Buchan novelized), a king who lived forever and had a magic mirror so that he could see every part of his territory at a glance. And if practical men such as Samuel Baker knew this was rubbish, the question remained – what *did* live at the equatorial heart of Africa?

Africa was certainly on Baker's mind from 1855 when he returned home from Ceylon. Valentine, soon to purchase his majority in the 10th Hussars, had served with the 12th Lancers in the Kaffir War (the eighth Cape War, 1852–53), so he had African experience himself, and talk of hunting elephants was joy to Samuel. Valentine's experiences against the fierce Basuto tribesmen had given him his first taste of military action before he sailed for the Crimea. Samuel wrote to Stuart-Wortley, now Lord Wharncliffe, asking him, in an age of networking, to put in a word for him to Lord Clarendon, the foreign secretary, who would have the final say in who would join Dr David Livingstone's plans to explore the Zambezi. Wharncliffe pulled out all the stops, extolling Baker's resourcefulness, his skills as writer, hunter, botanist and geologist, and stressed his enormous physical strength – just the sort of man to back Livingstone in a crisis.

Clarendon passed Wharncliffe's letter to Sir Roderick Murchison, president of the Geographical Society. And there Baker's dreams came to a full stop. The Geographical Society of London (it became Royal by charter in 1859) had begun life as an intellectual gentlemen's club in 1830, and – interestingly, bearing in mind Baker's new absorption – had incorporated the Association for Promoting the Discovery of the Interior Parts of Africa set up by Joseph Banks in 1788. Expeditions funded by the government via this body had all the status (and relative financial clout) of the space programme today. They were front-page news.

Murchison felt that Baker's credentials were insufficient. He talked to Livingstone and decided that Baker was merely a 'Nimrod' (hunter) and his joining the Zambezi operation 'out of the question'. Undeterred, Baker went directly to the society, proposing his own separate expedition from Walfish Bay in the company of his friends. The trip would last for two years and he would provide £2,000 of his own money. Eventually the decision was made that a second expedition might antagonize the Portuguese colonists in Mozambique (no one considered black Africans' views, of course) and make life difficult for Livingstone – presumably by upstaging him.

In the meantime, the exploratory grass was growing under Baker's feet. Two officers whom Baker knew well, John Hanning Speke and Richard Francis Burton, were already in Africa looking for the lakes that the second-century geographer Ptolemy had written about. Bayard Taylor, an American writer who had travelled up the Nile to the Sudan, south of Egypt, wrote: 'Since Columbus first looked upon San Salvador, the Earth has but one emotion of triumph left in her bestowal and that she reserves for him who shall first drink from the fountains of the White Nile, under the snow-fields of Kilimanjaro.'[2]

It was while Baker was at Constanza in 1859 that he first saw British newspaper accounts of the travels of Speke and Burton. Speke was Baker's junior by six years (Baker would reach forty by the time he travelled the Nile) and the son of a West Country cavalry officer. His schooling was limited because of latent tubercular problems which affected his eyesight, and he certainly did not have Baker's flair for writing or facility for learning languages. In 1844 he had joined the 46th Native Bengal Infantry, one of the regiments of the East India Company, and fought in both Sikh wars in the same decade. With peace in 1849, Speke became bored with soldiering and took to hunting in Tibet, sharing Baker's enthusiasm for 'sport'. In 1854, he met Richard Burton.

Burton hailed from Torquay, although his father owned estates in Hertfordshire. Colonel Joseph Burton had blotted his copybook (as did several army officers) by siding with Queen Caroline of Brunswick in her unseemly squabble with George IV in 1821. Accordingly, soon after Richard's birth, three months before Baker's, the family moved to the continent, where the boy spent most of his childhood. His father intended him, bizarrely given his later inclinations, for the Church, and he did well at Trinity College, Oxford, before being sent down for one too many unauthorized steeplechase outings. In 1842 Burton's father bought him a commission in the 18th Bombay Infantry, where his skill in languages (he spoke fluent Gujarati and Hindustani) made him a natural as a staff officer. Before he left India he had mastered over forty languages and dialects. His dark hair and swarthy looks enabled him to pass himself off as a native – his brother officers habitually referred to him as 'the white nigger' – and he often went among locals as Mirza Abdullah of Bushehr, half Iranian, half Arab. In something that sounds like a boy's own adventure, Burton operated as an undercover agent under General Charles Napier in suppressing infanticide, wife murder and male brothels in the newly conquered area of Scinde.

Back home in England in 1849, Burton wrote a number of books – like Baker's, instant bestsellers – on Scinde and its peoples. Three years later Burton suggested to the Geographical Society that he go on the *haj*, the Islamic pilgrimage to Mecca which was forbidden to non-Muslims. He went via Egypt, perfecting his Arabic and calling himself Sheikh Abdullah, a Sufi dervish who was also a doctor. He fasted during Ramadan and got to Medina, after hair-raising adventures, and went on to Mecca, where he prayed at the Kaaba[3] on 11 September 1853. The subsequent book he wrote put him at the forefront of English travellers.

Burton's next venture would bring him together with Speke. He wanted to go (as the first European to do so) to the forbidden city of Harar in Somalia. One of the team to go with him, Assistant Surgeon J.E. Stocks, died and was replaced by Lieutenant Speke. At the last minute the local resident, Sir James Outram, vetoed the trip as being too dangerous, and the party broke up to explore safer areas of Africa. Speke was sent to the gold hills of Wadi Nogal, while Burton went on alone to Harar. Here he posed as a British spy, banking on the fact that the amir (ruler) would not dare upset the world's leading naval power. He was right, but was glad to leave after ten days.

It was while planning the next expedition, to find the source of the White Nile, that disaster struck. The team had met up again at Berbera in April 1855, and were attacked by hostile natives. Speke had had a particularly hard time of it. His lack of experience and lack of languages meant that he blundered into local politics and tried to shout his way out, as many Englishmen did before and after him, in English. He had not found the gold he was looking for, and in the attack by the Har Owel tribe was wounded and captured. Lieutenant William Strogan of the Indian navy was killed in the clash and Burton skewered through his left cheek by a native spear.

The scar stayed with him all his life. Although Speke escaped, his excitable manner struck Burton as a mark of cowardice, the first sign of trouble between the exploration partners which would erupt again.

Both men then sailed for the Crimea. Burton, with the rank of captain and his Turkish language ability, served with the Bashi-Bazouks, the irregular cavalry that Baker would rather not work with. They were too unruly to form a regular battle force, and by 1855 a disillusioned Burton was back home. Speke also joined the Turkish contingent, but, like Burton, could not wait for the next African adventure.

I have dealt at some length with this pair because they (especially Burton) represented formidable rivals to Samuel Baker. Whereas he was turned down as a mere hunter, Burton had been presented with a gold medal by the Geographical Society, and was a force to be reckoned with.

East Africa by the late 1850s was becoming more important to Europe generally and Britain in particular. Although it would be twelve years in the making, the Suez Canal was an Anglo-French project commissioned in the new 'entente cordiale' atmosphere of the Crimean War and a need to cut trans-global travelling time. The route of the canal lay alongside East Africa, and the clashes between Arab slavers and black Africans there were increasing in number and severity.

Now both promoted to captaincies, Burton and Speke, financed by the Geographical Society, left Zanzibar in June 1857. Both suffered badly from malaria and related fevers, and Speke virtually went blind. When a beetle crawled into his inner ear he was obliged to cut it out with a knife, which left him permanently deaf. They somehow reached Lake Tanganyika in February 1858, and while Burton stayed there, unable to travel further, Speke went on to a further reported lake. Most of their 100 bearers had now deserted, having stolen vital equipment or broken it. At Tabora, an Arab slave port, Burton fell into a coma – it would be nearly a year before he could walk again. When conscious he worked on a treatise on local customs.

Speke went on without Burton and discovered the lake he named for Victoria. It was the source of the Nile, although Speke could not actually prove that. On his return he was so ill that without Burton he would probably have died. On 22 March 1859 they sailed for Aden. Here, Burton rested again, and Speke sailed home, promising to say nothing of the discoveries until Burton could join him.

In the event, Speke could not hold back and had already lectured to the Geographical Society before Burton got to England. Although Burton uncharacteristically held his tongue, it was obvious that Speke's claims to have discovered the Nile's source rankled. A more generous man would have acknowledged Burton's contribution, and Burton was genuinely uncertain whether Speke was correct in his claim.

As Samuel Baker began to formulate his own plans for African exploration, the rift between Burton and Speke became one of the most talked about head-on clashes in scholastic circles. It even dwarfed the public debates of the Darwinist Charles Huxley against the Bible-clinging Bishop 'Soapy Sam' Wilberforce in 1860.

While Burton went off in a huff to America and Canada in April 1860, Speke was sent back by the now Royal Geographical Society to prove his Lake Victoria findings. He was given £2,500 from the government and another £1,200 in public subscription. Captain James Augustus Grant, former tiger hunter and fellow Indian Army officer, would be his Burton for this trip.

'Nile fever' was gripping Britain when Samuel Baker came home in May, ostensibly to wind up his contract with the Danube and Black Sea railway. His ulterior motive was to launch his own African adventure, hoping to meet up with Speke somewhere in the dark continent. Speke had already sailed from Portsmouth on 27 April, but Baker had no intention of travelling with him. Instead, he let everyone believe he simply wanted to go to Africa to shoot elephants; after all, that was what he was famous for. He attended a 'Monday Evening at Home' at Room D4, Albany, a highly fashionable address in Piccadilly frequented by rich and often eccentric gentlemen. D4 was the apartment of Henry Murray, a retired admiral known by all and sundry as 'the skipper'. He had, as a contemporary noted, 'a mixture of bluffness' and 'almost womanly gentleness and courtesy'. He believed in flogging, and had a set of parallel bars in his pied-à-terre which he would encourage his (exclusively male) visitors to use.

One of the guests that particular evening was William Oswell, who had travelled with Livingstone on the Upper Zambezi. Oswell was keen on Baker's plans and lent him a No. 10 double-barrelled shotgun. Murray lent him a naval telescope.

Starting out from Constanza, Baker now began to write a series of letters to key people. He wrote to Burton (who was by now in Canada) and to Roderick Murchison, laying his plans before the Geographical Society on 20 November 1860. He intended to explore the desert areas of the Sudan, following as far as possible the White Nile from the north until he could get no further. He asked for maps and various scientific instruments. All this probably struck the society as rather too late. After all, Speke had done it ... hadn't he? Baker's argument of course was that no one had done it from the *north*. In other words, there was a piece of the geographical jigsaw missing.

The Geographical Society, however, was a closed shop – 'Mr Baker is not a Fellow of the Society and declined to become one when asked.' They did give him some guidelines, if no actual help, but played down any suggestion of meeting up with Speke, the darling of the hour. Baker was fully committed by this time: 'I had not the presumption to publish my intentions, as the sources of the Nile had hitherto defied all explorers, but I had inwardly determined to accomplish this difficult task or to die in the attempt'[4] – as Burton and Speke nearly had.

Another contact Baker had made at Albany was John Petherick, a Welshman who had lived in Egypt and the Sudan for fifteen years before being given the official title of consul for the Sudan. An engineer by training, he was, like Baker, a crack shot and keen hunter, and traded ivory south-west of Khartoum. Petherick intended to make the same journey that Baker did, meeting up with Speke, but he dithered for months in London, buying himself new guns and actively searching for a wife. This would have involved getting himself invited to the balls and soirées of the great and good during 'the Season', which ran from May to September, and was a sophisticated cattle market for young women of a marriageable age to find suitable men.[5] How suitable John Petherick was, with his huge beard and 'Africa' ways, is debatable. The

71

diminutive Lord John Russell, the foreign secretary, likened him to a hippopotamus.

Unlike virtually every other explorer, of Africa or elsewhere, Baker took his wife with him. This was partly because he could not leave her anywhere – she had no family left, and his did not know she existed. And I suspect it was also because Flooey insisted. The events of those weeks were written as a diary in an old journal from his Ceylon days, in two columns, writing from the back. Florence is referred to as 'F' throughout, perhaps, as Michael Brander suggests, so that in the event of his death and the diaries being found, 'F' would be presumed to be male and there would be no embarrassment caused to his family. Most of the comments in it are still those of the big-game hunter rather than the explorer.

Having arranged a sizeable transfer of funds to a bank in Alexandria, he and Florence left Cairo at dawn on 15 April 1861. They sailed up the Nile in a *diahbiah*, a large dhow, with little equipment. Baker had a firman or passport[6] from the Egyptian consul, Robert Colquhoun, whom Baker had last met in Bucharest, and who did not approve of the Bakers' unmarried status. Baker had a cook who was 'dirty and incapable' and a dragoman, Mahomet, a fixer whose supposed linguistic skills were appallingly limited.

The expedition stopped at Luxor, as tourists had done for half a century by this time, to take in the architectural wonders of Thebes. At Aswan, naked boys climbed aboard the boat, demanding backsheesh. 'How much young ladies must learn,' wrote Baker in his subsequent book, 'by a journey up the Nile which affords such opportunities for the study of human nature.'[7] He shot – and they ate – crocodile. 'The flavour of it,' Baker wrote, 'is between musky fish and the perspiration of a dirty person.' Florence watched the animal being cooked in a huge pot, one of its feet bubbling to the surface – 'it looked so human it made me shudder'.

Four weeks later, from Korosoko, the desert crossing began. Samuel's drawings, worked up by a better artist later, show Florence in a broad-brimmed wide-awake and veil, sitting pensively on her camel, and her husband in a kepi with neck flap, which was essential against the merciless sun. The temperature was 110°F in the shade. By this time, the Baker caravan consisted of sixteen camels, two servants and a vast amount of luggage. Florence became ill with exhaustion and the heat, and the expedition halted near Berbera to give her a rest.

Samuel presented his firman to the local governor and his predecessor, Haleem Effendi. The Bakers hugely enjoyed the cool of the shade, the trees and the cooing of ringdoves. Haleem was concerned about Baker's objective. Drinking coffee and smoking pipes, he warned of the dangers of tracing the source of the great river. The climate was deadly, and so were the black tribes to the south. And what about Mrs Baker? In July, Colquhoun wrote to his opposite number in Zanzibar, Christopher Rigby:

> Petherick takes with him a stout bucksome wife! He will be joined by a great friend of mine, whom perhaps you know, Samuel White Baker the Ceylon sportsman. He too takes up a charming little woman with him – I much fear both these ladies may lose health, perhaps life in their rambles.

Nothing could deter Baker, however, and before they left Berbera, the wives of the town's great and good visited them. Florence, who, like Sam, was still mastering Arabic, entertained them by showing them her clothes, sewing, china and the metal bedsteads in their tent. The *sitt* (lady of the English traveller) charmed them all. Baker noted in his diary how the Arab women squatted naked over a fire-pit and held their robes out to soak up burning incense so that they smelt fragrant.

The Bakers left three portmanteaux, seven packing cases and three barrels of gunpowder behind for Petherick, some weeks behind them, and followed the dried course of the Atbara river. The notes Samuel made now were much more what the Geographical Society expected of him: 'The river is as thick as pea soup and not only undrinkable but unwashable ... All water and likewise milk should be boiled in this country – fever lies in both.'

Baker bathed every day in the metal bath they carried and rode his way through a bout of malaria which had stopped Burton in his tracks. They now had two soldiers as guards and escorts. Baker noted – and shot – the wildlife. The shallow Atbara waters were home to huge crocodiles, turtles, fish and – a first for Baker – hippopotami. He killed his first one, found that it made excellent soup, and left the carcase for the local natives to help themselves.

This pattern of endearing himself to local tribes by providing meat for them was a good move and became more necessary the further south they travelled. Baker was horrified by the native custom of eating an animal's lungs, liver and kidneys raw as the hunters skinned the beast.

On 23 June the river suddenly burst into life, a flash flood driving the brown water cascading over the baked mud. The next day the water was 500 yards wide and 20 feet deep in places. Baker wrote excitedly: 'The rains were pouring in Abyssinia! These were the sources of the Nile.'[8] The expedition moved on to Cassala, 340 miles from Berbera. Baker shot wild asses but found the meat very disagreeable. Antelope skins were made into water canteens, and all animal fat was made into soap or candles or used for cooking. Baker noted the exact method and measurement for soap-making using potash and lime. Even before they reached Sofi, their next stop, Florence was laid low again with fever and had to be helped onto her camel. Baker was in his element. He was a brilliant, resourceful cook and could fix just about anything from a broken gun stock to a broken leg. In the villages through which they rode, he was taken for a *hakim*, a doctor, because of his medicine chest. The natives were particularly impressed with his liver pills and dyspepsia remedies. He was a 'master of their bowels, as I set them going and stop them at will'. When a hunter named Jali was brought to him with a snapped thigh after an elephant trod on him, Baker rigged up splints from tree branches, and Florence made bandages 200 feet long to act as a cast. This was soaked in gum from the mimosa tree, and Jali was sent home on top of a camel on a bed Baker had made for him. In six weeks the man was hunting again.

Samuel's clothes, made by Florence, were a variant of his Ceylon gear. He wore shorts gathered in at the knee and a short-sleeved shirt, the cotton dyed with mimosa fruit a khaki brown. His gaiters of gazelle skin protected his legs from the murderous thorns of the Sudan scrub. He made his shoes himself from gazelle hide, so they were light and durable.

At Sofi the Bakers bought a house for 2 shillings and had it transported to their camp by the river on the heads of thirty bearers. Here was 'perfect immunity from all Poor Rates, tithes, taxes and other public burdens and not more than 2,000 miles from a church'.

Baker wrote drily that the single circular room, 14 feet in diameter, was at once entrance hall, dining room, drawing room, ladies' boudoir, library, breakfast room, bedroom and dressing room. 'The architecture was of an ancient style from an original design of a pillbox surmounted by a candle extinguisher.' He listed ten guns, including the one lent by Oswell. The Fletcher No. 24 was the only one light enough for Florence to use, and she became a good shot with it. His 'Baby', the elephant gun he had had made years before by Holland of Bond Street, was called *Jemma el Mootfah* – child of a cannon – by the Arabs.

There were problems obtaining servants. 'These Arabs,' wrote Baker, wholly in tune with every other travelling Englishman of his generation, 'are the most lying, perfidious, dirty scoundrels on God's earth. They are all alike, therefore it is no use kicking the posterior of any individual.' Kick them he did, however, and box their ears when they transgressed. It was the Arab way, too. He gave one servant the money to make his *haj* to Mecca, and took to the boy Bacheet the Bakers hired in Casalla. Bacheet was a good bearer, but had no idea of table manners. Flies were a major problem, especially at mealtimes, and Bacheet would pick out the wriggling creatures – which, according to Baker, committed suicide in their thousands by diving into his tea and coffee – with his fingers. Baker taught him to use a teaspoon for this, having wiped it carefully first, and then laughed uproariously when the 'ignoramus' used the same technique (and spoon) to fish the flies out of the Bakers' chamber pot.

On 15 September the whole camp crossed the Atbara to the better shooting country on the far bank. Their entourage had grown by now. They had two servant boys and an old slave woman they called Sarah, as well as Mahomet. When Baker shot edible animals he would hoist the Union flag over his house (moved across bit by bit on the bath) and let the natives help themselves.

Sofi itself had recently been a war zone, and there was a long history of belligerency between the Abyssinian locals and the Egyptian authorities, but there were also some Europeans there, and the Bakers made friends with them. One was a stonemason, Florian Mouche, who had come out with a party of Austrian missionaries, but had turned to hunting and selling live animals to the new zoos which were springing up all over Europe. His guns were poor and he had blown his thumb off using one. His African servant had hacked the digit clean, and Baker told him that if a European surgeon had been involved he would have lost the whole hand. Johann Schmidt was a carpenter who had likewise deserted the missionaries, and spent happy days talking to the Bakers in his native German.

Baker's diary in those five months at Sofi is full of natural history. He drew, described and measured the animals he saw and shot, noting that monkeys worked together as teams: 'If a monkey could only light a fire he would be a reasonable animal.' Florence had a pet monkey called Wallady, and a tame toad lived in one of Samuel's shoes, waddling out occasionally to eat flies and be stroked. Baker even dissected animals, noting the contents of a bustard's stomach – scorpions, ants, beetles and a lizard.

His observations of the Arabs are fascinating. He could be down-right wrong in his conclusions – 'Great doctors are the Arabs – dogs are treated for distemper by being thrown from the top of the house to the ground' – not taking into account the huge contribution of Arab medicine in the medieval world which actually added to what he knew.

Baker came into contact with a variety of nomadic or semi-nomadic tribes – the Bedouin, Hadendowas and Bishareens. He was hugely impressed by Achmet abou Sinn, the sheikh of the Shook-erijahs. He was 6 feet 3 inches (taller than Baker in that land of short men), and at 80 'as erect as a lance'. This grand old man had warned the Bakers of moving further south, especially in the rainy season when the sand turned to mud. Unable to shake the travellers' resolve, he gave them two *hygeens*, near-white riding camels, and an escort under the command of his grandson.

The slave woman Sarah was hired for $1 a month. This was the Austrian thaler, impressed with the head of the eighteenth-century empress Maria Theresa, and widely used as currency in that part of Africa. Sarah's daughter was 18 years old. 'This woman's love for her daughter,' Baker wrote, 'is delightful to witness; her daughter is the moon in her long night of slavery. Without her, all were dark and hopeless.' Perhaps he was quietly missing his own daughters; Edith would be 13 by now and he had not seen her for six years.[9]

In this land of slavery, Baker bought a servant girl of the Galla tribe, Barrake, for £7. He had of course bought her freedom, but Barrake interpreted this as a marriage proposal (in this land of many wives) and leapt on him, smothering him with kisses as she wrapped her castor-oil-lacquered hair around him. She was disappointed when Mahomet explained the reality of the situation. Baker noted that the slave girls were beautiful but not strong enough for hard work or expeditions. 'Their forms are peculiarly elegant and graceful,' and they were proud and quick learners. Europeans living in Khartoum married girls like this. They washed clothes by dancing naked on them at the riverbank, and the vaginas of little girls were partially sewn up to ensure chastity and to give future husbands greater satisfaction. The stitching was only undone for childbirth. Florence actually witnessed this 'circumcision' ceremony taking place, and it made her physically ill. She was as much appalled by the fact that mothers acquiesced in the whole procedure as she was by the physical cruelty involved.

What fascinated Baker most, however, was the Aggageers, the elephant hunters of the Hamran tribe. These men chased elephants on horseback: as one distracted the beast by riding backwards and forwards in front of him, others dismounted and advanced on foot, bringing the enraged animal down by hacking at its hamstrings with their two-handed swords. African elephants were bigger than Indian and more difficult to stop, as Baker found out when he fired 'Baby' at one. The gun's recoil almost broke his nose, and he could manage only five kills a day because of the extraordinary thickness of the elephants' skulls. Florian Mouche managed only one with his inferior weapon, and Baker warned him to buy a new one. Two years later, when his gun misfired, Mouche was killed by a lion he was hunting.

Baker revelled in his hunts with the Hamran, who were as impressed with him as he was with them. Moving south he saw and killed his first lions and rhinoceros, and hunted with the local tribal leader Sheikh Abou Do Roussal. Baker became disillusioned with this man. 'Though a perfect Nimrod in sport, an Apollo in appearance', he was also mean, grasping and jealous. For the sake of a peaceful coexistence, Baker learned to let the man be first to a kill. The Sheriff brothers were more generous, and Baker marvelled at one of them, Roder, who had a withered left arm and yet still took a full part in the elephant hunt.

It was easy, as Speke had found, to upset locals, whose ways and traditions were so different from those of the Europeans. When Abou Do tried to sell Schmidt a rhino calf worth $40 for a zoo, Baker pointed out that the animal had been strangled by the cords that bound it to a camel and that no one would pay anything for a dead calf. A furious Abou Do accused Baker of killing the animal with his 'evil eye'.

Barrake the slave girl died of dysentery, and the dragoman Mahomet deserted. As the party neared the dangerous country of the Basé tribe, and the psychopathic tribal leader Mek Nimmur (the leopard king), the bearers understandably grew nervous and pleaded sickness. Baker gave them tartar emetic so they really were ill and could not leave. He then stood at the camp entrance with his double-barrelled rifle under his arm and threatened to shoot the first camel that left (and quite possibly the rider with it). No one else deserted.

In fact, the meeting with Mek Nimmur could not have been more cordial. The king sent a magnificently white-robed musician to Baker's camp, carrying an umbrella, two pistols and a *rababa* (a sort of violin). 'He sang to me,' wrote Baker, 'as though I had been Richard Coeur de Lyon,' and the explorer was expected to pay for the song. When, a few hours later, a similarly clad musician turned up, Baker sent him packing. Mek Nimmur himself was dirty and very much on the run. He kept a saddled horse near him at all times. He was obviously suffering, Baker realized, from syphilis. Baker gave him a brace of pistols and when he heard, to his embarrassment, that one of these had exploded, he sent him a rifle in compensation.

By early April 1861, a year after they had set out, the Bakers were making for Khartoum, at the meeting of the Blue and White Niles. Baker had studied the tributaries of the Blue Nile, noting down everything he thought would interest the Geographical Society. But by now everybody was tetchy. The flies and the heat were unbearable. Bacheet had sunstroke. The locals were unfriendly and even the few Europeans they met disagreeable. One German annoyed

Baker with his views on the appalling behaviour of the Jews in the Sudan.

When they reached Khartoum they heard news that John Petherick and his new wife had gone south in search of Speke, of whom there was still no word. Petherick's consulate was at the Bakers' disposal in his absence, and they found it a menagerie, with ostriches strutting around the courtyard. A wild boar had escaped from its cage and charged the Bakers on the veranda. Samuel saw it off with a well-aimed stone, something of a miracle because the crack shot with a rifle was anything but with any other kind of missile. As Dorothy Middleton writes: 'The only really safe animal at the consulate was the British lion over the door.'

The Bakers received letters here. In family news, Valentine was now lieutenant colonel of the 10th Hussars. In other news, a civil war was under way in America over slavery and state rights. And Prince Albert of Saxe-Coburg-Gotha, consort of Queen Victoria, was dead from typhoid. Perhaps even at this early stage in his career as an explorer, an idea came to Samuel White Baker.

Chapter 8

The Lake of Dead Locusts

'The springs of the Nile flow between the two mountains, Croplii and Mophi and these springs are bottomless, half the water flows to Egypt and the north, the other half towards Ethiopia and the south.' This was the view of the Greek historian Herodotus, and it was up to a handful of Englishmen nearly twenty-five centuries later to prove him right or wrong. Today the Nile is still a remarkable river, tamed as it has been by dams and hydraulic systems. Robert Collins wrote: 'The river bubbles from remote springs in Burundi and Ethiopia and it descends over falls and rapids and through swamps and plains to make the longest journey of any river in the world, more than 4,230 miles, before emptying into the Mediterranean Sea.'[1]

Samuel Baker's greatest challenge now lay before him. By the time he and Florence reached Khartoum in summer 1861 they both spoke quite fluent Arabic, which was to be vital in that they were now almost wholly dependent on the 'Turks' (actually Egyptians) who were to guide them further south towards the equator. Khartoum itself was barely thirty years old when the Bakers got there. Standing at the confluence of the Blue and White Niles, it had been built by the Albanian Mehemet Ali. The city was run by the 'Turks' (actually Circassians or Armenians), but like any large settlement in Africa, it was full of Europeans (like Petherick) looking out for any angle they could find. In the 1860s most of them were hunters or ivory traders, but a significant minority made money out of the slave trade.

Baker's diary explains that he found most Sudanese were 'saucy' and quarrelsome, but he admired many of them. One sheikh was 85, ate two pounds of butter a day and had just married his latest bride, a 14-year-old girl. 'There may be a hint for the octogenarians,'

Baker wrote; presumably he was referring to the butter intake.[2] Another had a habit of blowing his nose on his fingers before smearing mucus all over the wall. He spat under his carpet too. His banquets, however, were magnificent.

Khartoum had mosques and a huge Coptic Christian church, a governor's palace and an army barracks. The name means 'elephant's tusk', describing the landspit between the rivers on which it was built, and of course referring to the place's major economy, ivory. In Europe this was made into parasol handles, billiard balls and bowls and the hilts of generals' swords, where Victorians believed it looked more attractive than on the animal which originally owned it. Animal skins which graced European libraries and trophy rooms were also brought to Khartoum by the hunters, and there was a huge trade in ostrich feathers, especially in Britain, where the thriving 'death business' used thousands of black plumes a year.[3]

Baker was initially annoyed that the French had a large foothold in Khartoum. Lording it over everybody else was Georges Thibault, a white hunter and animal trader who had been there for forty years. He had brought the first giraffes to Britain, parading them from London docks to the zoo as the locals looked on in their thousands, open-mouthed. The French may have been Britain's allies in the Crimea, but that hardly undid a history of enmity, and in the clash of interests between the two countries in the Sudan we see the first glimmers of the 'scramble for Africa' that became potentially deadly by the 1890s.[4]

Richard Hall makes the point that Baker was probably glad the Pethericks had gone so that he did not have to explain Florence to them. Since the consulate was now being run in their absence by a housekeeper who was formerly John Petherick's mistress, it would seem the Welshman did not actually have a leg to stand on.

The news of Petherick's party was not good. He was looking for Speke and Grant, accompanied by his wife, Katharine, and two naturalists – the Scot James Murie and the American Clarence Bronnell. The winds from the south made his navigation of the river frustratingly slow and much time was lost as the crews had to drag their boats by rope from the banks. Bronnell died of malaria.

Baker learned from a French traveller, Guillaume Lejean – whom he first despised, commenting in his diary, 'Looks vermin', but later came to admire and like – that the next 'settlement', if that was the word, was Gondokoro, reached ten years earlier by Austrian missionaries. The place had since been abandoned, however, as there was not a single convert among the local tribes, and the death toll among the priests was enormous. Instead, Gondokoro had become a slave post, inhabited for only a few months of the year while the Bari natives were caught and shipped upriver. 'The missionaries should have taken away their cross,' Lejean told Baker, 'for since they left it has only seen the scum of Khartoum.'

Neither Baker was impressed with Khartoum. It was filthy with dead animals left to rot in the streets, and male prostitution was rife, at the Turkish barracks as well as among the civilian population. Baker and Petherick were the only Europeans with white wives – the other thirty or so took several African concubines. They had not been in the city long when a new governor-general arrived with a retinue of 1,800 troops. He was Musa Pasha Hamdi, formerly a Circassian slave, and every bit as treacherous and unscrupulous as the slavers themselves.

Baker went to see him, showing the maps he had drawn of the Blue Nile tributaries and explaining that Mek Nimmur wanted to talk peace. Musa was not interested. It soon became obvious that the governor-general was being as obstructive as possible. It was widely known that the British hated slavery, and most Khartoumers probably regarded Baker as a spy. When he tried to buy mules for his expedition, Musa outbid him at auction. 'Well done dignity,' a furious Baker wrote, 'when the Governor General of the Sudan sells his own donkeys in public.'

The oddest Europeans in Khartoum were the 'Dutch ladies'. Even a maverick such as Baker was horrified that they were travelling alone (their male servants did not count) in such hostile country. Harriet Tinné was a 63-year-old widow and with her were her sister Adriana van Capellan, a spinster, and her daughter, the beautiful Alexandrine Tinné. All three were ridiculously rich, millionaires by today's standards; the source of their wealth, like Baker's, was the West Indian sugar trade. They were ripped off by all and sundry, especially the attentive Georges Thibault, who acted as their protector and middleman, bumping up prices and making a tidy profit for himself.

The ladies acquired the only steamship that far south on the Nile, spending an estimated 450,000 francs in the process. Harriet Tinné wrote of the Bakers: 'A famous English couple have arrived. Samuel and Florence Baker are going up the White Nile to find Speke. They have been travelling in Ethiopia and I hear she has shot an elephant! She wears trousers and gaiters and a belt and blouse. She goes everywhere he goes.'[5] The Tinnés had actually done Baker a disservice, because he now had to pay exorbitant sums for his expedition. He was concerned that they would rival his venture, and they were concerned that he would want to commandeer their steamer. In the event, they sailed north and he saluted them as they left from the banks of the Nile. All the Dutch ladies would be dead within the year, Alexandrine murdered by her camel drivers in the Sahara and the others from fever.

Baker's plan was to spend the time equipping his expeditions until October and to reach Gondokoro by the end of the following month. This was a pious hope; in Africa *everything* takes longer than expected. Baker sent letters to 'the skipper' in Albany, knowing the old gossip would pass on his news in the right circles. He also sent samples of raw cotton to the Royal Geographical Society. Now that the American Civil War was at its height, the Federal navy had blockaded the Confederate cotton ports, and although Baker cannot have known it, Lancashire, the home of cotton-spinning, was experiencing genuine economic hardship; an alternative supply might prove useful.

Baker learned in October that his father had died, and he felt guilty because he was the only one of his children not there at the end. By early December the expedition had recruited a forty-five man escort, which Baker attempted to drill as a private army. He even designed their khaki uniform and taught them rifle drill. He had twenty-one donkeys, four camels and four horses, and stores which included grain and trinkets for the tribes they would meet. Johann Schmidt arrived in time to join them, although in fact he was already dying from consumption (tuberculosis). Baker made a will, as death in the dark continent was a constant possibility. He left

84

ample money for Florence to get back to Europe, yet her status, as a woman alone and an ex-slave, was a constant worry to him.

On 18 December 1862, just as the party was about to sail, agents arrived from Musa demanding a tax on everyone on board the ships. Baker ran up the Union flag and told them he was neither Turkish nor a trader, and promising that if there was any more delay, he would throw them into the Nile. That seemed to do the trick. As they travelled south, through countryside that was flat and monotonous, they were plagued by mosquitoes – 'the nightingales of the Nile' – and the aptly-named boat *The Clumsy* caused delays with a weak mast. By 4 January, Baker was convinced that all of Africa must be one vast swamp – the sudd of the southern Sudan – and his men had to bend their backs hauling the boats from the bank. Baker and Florence both succumbed to recurring bouts of fever, probably malaria, and sensibly moored the boats in mid-river where the mosquito swarms were slightly less.

They spent a miserable Christmas as Schmidt's condition worsened. Water hyacinths clogged their passage. Tall papyrus waved overhead, reminding Baker in the months ahead, when Florence came close to death, of the nodding plumes of funerals. On New Year's Eve, Johann Schmidt died. He had talked for days with Florence in German, but much of it was rambling and punctuated by coughing up blood. 'Ich bin sehr dankbar' ('I am very grateful') were his last words, and Baker buried him under a tamarind tree by moonlight.

Throughout this journey, the Bakers' retinue showed constant signs of wavering, even, on at least two occasions, outright mutiny. With a combination of Florence's persuasion and Baker's right hook, they managed to hold the 'army' together. Only two of the servants could be trusted to stay loyal. One was Richarn, Schmidt's man, and the other was a 12-year-old missionary boy called Saat. The lad had turned up one day and knelt beside Florence, begging to be taken with the trip. As he was an orphan and the Austrian mission had collapsed by this time, the Bakers took pity on him. Florence regarded him as a son, making his clothes and teaching him the English she herself was still learning. He could eat for Egypt, but Baker wrote of him: 'We were very fond of this boy; he was thoroughly good.'

Samuel drew and made notes on the tribes they encountered that January. The Dinka in particular were made ugly by their custom of ornamenting their upper lips. He was horrified to learn that the men used spiked bracelets to beat their wives into submission. 'I have never pitied poor creatures more than these destitute savages. Their method of thanking you for anything is by spitting on your hand.'

Baker used the noonday sun to calculate their position as they travelled. By the middle of January they were 6° 39' north of the equator, and they reached the almost abandoned Austrian mission station of St Croix on the 23rd. By this time, the Bakers' party was travelling more or less in conjunction with the boats of the slaver Kurshid Aga, and it was a fascinating snapshot moment when the lay missionary Franz Morlang, pledged to remove slavery from the Sudan, sold the mission station to his implacable enemy for £30. There were probably those at home, in both Austria and Britain, who would mutter about thirty pieces of silver, but men such as Morlang and Baker had to live through Africa. Armchair geographers and do-gooders such as the British Anti-Slavery Society had no idea.

Over a few glasses of wine, Baker learned that in fact the whole Austrian mission on the Nile was a front by Franz Josef to establish a Habsburg colony there, another example of the growing scramble for Africa.

Gondokoro, when they reached it on 2 February, was 'a perfect hell', far dirtier than Khartoum. It was just a cluster of camps where quarrels were rife and the sound of musket fire common. A boy on one of the Bakers' boats was killed by an apparently random shot soon after their arrival. On the other hand it could have been a calculated warning. Most of the slaves were hidden away once the white couple arrived, and their coming was not welcome. Baker had half expected Speke or at least Petherick to be there, but there was no sign of either. There was a ruined church (the remains of a mission) and a solitary brick-built ruin. Baker was appalled to find one of the slavers flying the American flag.[6]

Baker decided to wait for Speke. The man was now a full year behind his known schedule, but if he were alive, surely his arrival would be imminent. In the meantime Baker made notes of the poisoned arrows of the natives, and was glad that their inelastic bows had such limited range.

It was now that trouble erupted. Baker's men had been 'got at' by the men in the camps and asked permission to go on a cattle raid, both a traditional African pastime and a means of improving diet. Baker refused, and the ringleader began to berate him. Baker ordered the man to be whipped. The men now became an angry, milling mob, armed with sticks, and the ringleader aimed a blow at him. Baker caught the stick and knocked the man down with a right hook. Florence, ill in bed but hearing the commotion, used a great deal of tact and poise in asking Samuel to spare the man. On Baker's orders, a drummer boy beat to quarters and the line fell in.

Baker knew perfectly well that he was heavily outnumbered. Apart from himself, he had a small woman in her twenties, a black servant and a 12-year-old boy. So he enlisted the help of the slaver Kurshid Aga, whose boats had been trailing the Bakers' from Khartoum. Baker bought three oxen from him and treated his wavering men to a feast. It was bribery, of course, but sound psychology. It was also unlikely to last for long.

On the morning of 15 February, gunfire from across the desert heralded the arrival of a new party. It was Speke and Grant, in the company of a group under the Italian trader Andrea de Bono which had left days before. Baker ran along the shore, waving his sun hat. Speke was astonished. He had not seen Baker for nearly ten years, since their meeting on a steamship out of Aden, and had never seen him with a beard. He assumed at first that it was Petherick of whom he had seen no sign. 'What a joy it was,' wrote Speke, 'I can scarcely tell ... old friend Baker, famed for his sports in Ceylon ... We could not talk fast enough.'

Speke's story sounded all too familiar to Baker. He could not rely on his interpreters (at least the Bakers spoke Arabic), but he once again found himself caught up in the political minefield of relations between the Arabs, most of whom were slave-traders, and the black tribes they preyed upon. It had taken Speke and Grant ten months to reach Lake Victoria from the coast. Speke's questioning the native kings and chiefs about Petherick's whereabouts and boats from the north led some of them to believe that an invasion by the white men might be imminent, so they delayed incessantly.

James Augustus Grant, Speke's right-hand man, was a former Indian Army officer who had lost a thumb with the 78th Highlanders at Lucknow during the Indian Mutiny. He accompanied Speke on what Lord Palmerston called a 'long walk', but a badly ulcerated leg meant separation from Speke for several weeks. He had taken photographic equipment with him to record the expedition, but the heat and blinding sun soon made this useless, and he fell back on his considerable drawing skills: 147 sketches still survive, as well as Grant's 320-page journal. Once again, force of circumstance meant that Speke went on alone, as he had with Burton, to the point where the lake emptied into the river. This he called the Ripon Falls. Unlike the Burton situation, there would be no open rift between Speke and Grant, but likewise, without corroboration of Speke's account, it would take twelve years before his claims could be verified.

But all this lay in the future. For now, the African explorers were glad to have met up. The northern expedition had met the southern, and the Nile, as Speke told a rapturous press and public at home some months later, 'was settled'.

There was one awkward moment. Grant wrote in a letter years later that when Speke met Florence he said, 'I thought your wife was dead.' Baker introduced Florence to Grant as 'ma chere amie', a euphemism that said it all. The explorers, together with the missionary Franz Morlang, who joined them briefly before returning to Khartoum, discussed the significance of their finds. Speke had formed the impression that the Buranda tribe around the lake, tall and handsome, were some sort of African aristocracy, streets ahead of other tribes and perhaps the so-called lost tribe of Israel. This nonsense plagued anthropologists for years to come. The Buranda king, Mutesa, was an overlord to lesser tribes. At his coronation dozens of tribesmen had been virtually stoned to death, and if one of his many wives displeased him, he would have her strangled. He was fascinated by Speke's guns, and had the explorer shoot a cow each morning to prove how they worked.

Speke was not fond of John Petherick. When the latter and his seriously ill wife reached Gondokoro on 20 February, he was cold-shouldered by Speke, who pointedly refused any of the cash and supplies Petherick had from the Geographical Society and the

Samuel Baker on his return from the governor-generalship of the Sudan, wearing Sudanese dress. The natives called him Malaggé ('man with a beard').

Florence Baker on her return from the Sudan in 1873, about 32 years old. Natives would remember her years later as the Morning Star.

A hippopotamus rams the Bakers' *diahbiah* on the Nile. These animals were highly dangerous especially at night, and Baker is reaching for his gun. Florence appears to be shouting back at the hippo.

The engineers brought the steamers in sections across the desert, with the help of bearers and 1,00 camels.

nuel Baker (in the foreground) leads his 'Forty Thieves' against the slavers at Fatiko.

erever the Bakers went, they set the slaves free. In the foreground, an engineer smashes off their ckles, while Samuel and Julian organize the liberation. Note Florence with the children.

APOSTLES OF LIBERTY.

Wilberforce to Sir S. Baker. RECEIVE A NATION'S THANKS, WITH MINE, FOR FIGHTING FREEDOM'S CAUSE,

Samuel Baker as the Apostle of Liberty from *Judy* magazine. William Wilberforce, the great anti-slaver, is shown congratulating him.

Baker of the Tenth. Valentine Baker in the uniform of lieutenant colonel of the 10th Hussars – the man on the white horse.

Headquarters of the Royal Geographical Society in Savile Row, which did not sponsor Baker's expedition because he was not a member. (*Eloise Campbell*)

Samuel Baker lectures to the Royal Geographical Society on his triumphal return from the sources of the Nile. The meeting was held in a new London University building to house the large numbers in the audience. Sitting second from Baker's left is Bartle Frere, the society's president.

The last official photograph of Samuel Baker, taken at Sandford Orleigh, 1892.

The governor general and his retinue. Whenever the Bakers – Samuel, Florence and Julian – arrived in a new area, they and the 'Forty' wore their full dress uniforms.

government. The sparkly Kate Petherick was barely recognizable, her mind temporarily wandering and her clothes in rags. Petherick had been totally unable to control his bearers and they had gone on cattle raids and added to the size of the expedition by picking up black slave girls. The doctor, Murie, had been obliged to boil the heads of three blacks killed in a fight. He turned this into an anatomical exercise by having the skulls sent for study by the Royal College of Surgeons back in London.

The vengeful Speke destroyed Petherick's reputation when he got home in May 1863, which makes it all the more odd that he lent all his maps and notes to Baker. In all the excitement of the meeting, the twinge of disappointment was that the job was done: Speke and Grant had, in effect, beaten Samuel Baker to it. 'Does not one leaf of the laurel remain for me?' he asked Speke. The leaf was the Luta N'zige, the Dead Locust, a lake that reportedly lay to the west of the Victoria and that the Nile ran through. Neither Speke nor Grant had had the time or energy to explore it, or even verify its existence.

On 25 February, Speke and Grant sailed north to Khartoum in the Bakers' boat. The idea now was that Baker and Petherick would join forces and head south, but Petherick was a marked man. He had already offended the Arabs by arresting two high-profile slavers in Khartoum, and he had offended Speke by not providing the support he had promised. Dejectedly, the Pethericks returned to Khartoum to salvage what they could of 'Pett's' career, and the Bakers sailed on.

It was at this point that a second mutiny occurred. The natives knew that they were heading into the territory of another psychopathic king, Kamrasi, and beyond that the feared Mutesa, who strangled his own wives and had people shot for fun. In an event that sounds pure Victorian melodrama, the boy Saat overheard a plot against the Bakers, and Samuel was ready for it. At dawn, he had a bed placed outside his tent and laid six of his guns, loaded, on it. There was also a sabre for good measure. The men were ordered to assemble with the mackintosh covers over their gun locks. If any of the fifteen moved, Baker would shoot him on the spot. They backed down and Baker dismissed them, writing the word 'mutineer' on their discharge papers.

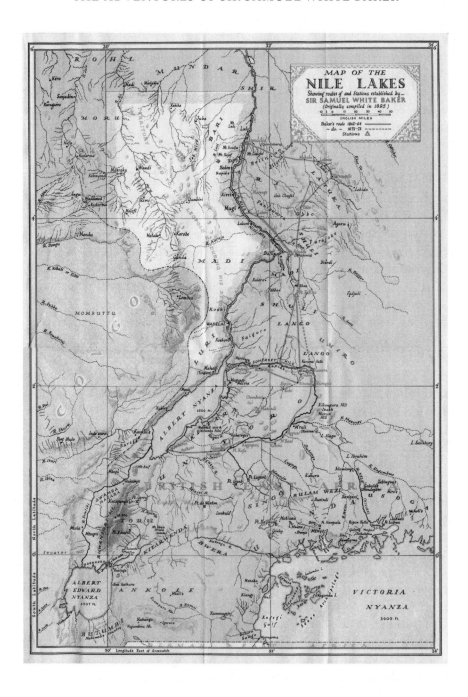

At last, by 26 March, the expedition was under way, the Bakers riding horses Tetch and Filful, and with seventeen of the slaver Kurshid's men as their escort. Dr James Murie shook hands with Baker and perhaps secretly did not expect to see him again.

It was on this stage of the journey that the Baker legend really grew. The natives referred to the Arabs as 'white men'; Baker was a 'very white man' and he took off his shirt to prove it. They called him Mlidju, the big-bearded. Florence, with her waist-length golden hair, was Rijadnay, white pearl or Njinyeri, the Morning Star. Usually wearing gaiters and breeches, she was believed by some of them to be a boy, perhaps Baker's son.

The going was tough. They had to move fast before the rains came, because the dried-up stream beds would become lethal torrents of foaming water impossible to cross. They had been travelling only a few days when they ran into an armed party of 140 men. Its leader was Ibrahim, a slaver who operated for Kurshid, and Florence asked him for help. Baker was less conciliatory. Warning that if any harm befell him or Florence the British would hang him in Khartoum, a sort of working relationship was set up. Baker's cash and a double-barrelled rifle sweetened the moment. Now Baker realized the pressures the Pethericks had been under. He could not stop Ibrahim's men stealing cattle and slave girls from the Latooka tribe through whose lands they marched. In one particularly grisly episode an intruder at the camp was shot by Ibrahim's guards. They wanted to torture him with their bayonets, but Baker prevented it. When the intruder was dead, the body was dragged into the bush and Baker watched transfixed as the vultures picked the skeleton clean, going first for the eyes, the underarms, the inner thighs.

When entering the territory of a new tribe, the Bakers invited the chief to join them. Florence wore a dress and Samuel usually his Atholl kilt. This was an expensive business – the chief and his numerous wives expected gifts. One of the wives was sketched by Baker, and she was astonished at the likeness. She told Florence (all this through an interpreter) how beautiful she was, but would look even better in local style with her four front teeth knocked out and an ornament placed in her lower lip. Her own was a glass and wire object, so Baker snapped a glass thermometer and gave the pieces to the chief's wife as a new ornament. It is not recorded how she coped with possible mercuric poisoning.

From Latooka country they reached the Obbo lands. Their chief Katchiba, father of 116 children, was a clown, singer and, like many African rulers, a shaman, famed for his rain-making abilities. Not for the first time Baker used a mixture of sangfroid and bluff. He whistled with his two fingers – something the Obbo had never experienced before – and as luck would have it, it rained four days later. Katchiba became the proud owner of the Bakers' tea service and a pair of goggles. He wanted their chamber pot, but when Samuel explained that this was a sacred vessel, Katchiba let the matter go. 'He is really not a bad fellow for a native,' Baker wrote, and was quite content to leave Florence in the chief's kraal while he went elephant hunting, something Queen Victoria was horrified by when she read of it years later.

Waiting for the rains to stop and the river levels to fall, Baker experimented with making red wine – brewed in the iron bath. The result was not wonderful – the whisky he made later from sweet potatoes was far more successful. Both Bakers fell ill while staying at the Obbo kraal, and Katchiba went into his witch-doctor routine, spitting water around their hut and waving a branch about. It seemed to work, despite the constant irritation of ants and rats in their quarters. 'White ants and rats, robbers and smallpox,' wrote a depressed Baker, 'these are my companions and neighbours.' One by one their horses and donkeys died, victims of the dreaded tsetse fly. They were replaced by oxen, which became tame enough to be stroked and tickled, but were sullen and unpredictable. At one stage on the march, both Bakers were thrown by them, and an increasingly ill Samuel had to undergo an exhausting stroll of eighteen hours. As the malaria returned with increasing frequency, supplies of quinine were running dangerously low. By the day after Boxing Day 1863, he could write only one word in his diary – 'Fever'.

When the rains stopped, the pair moved on, Baker noting latitudes, altitudes and other technical readings for the Geographical Society. They were moving now through the apparently endless swamp land that edged the kingdom of the feared Kamrasi. On 22 January 1864 they reached the Victoria White Nile which Speke had named the Somerset after his native county. 'Halted 80 feet above the river,' Baker wrote, 'altitudes above sea level by observation 3864 feet.'

The explorers found Kamrasi every bit as shifty and obstructive as Speke said he was. He was extraordinarily grasping, accepting with glee one of Baker's guns, a carpet, socks, shawls, necklaces, bracelets, even the yellow handkerchief with which Florence tied her hat on her head. In the end, the king came to the point: he wanted Florence herself and would happily exchange several of his own wives. Outraged, Baker pulled a revolver on the man and held it against his chest. If Kamrasi repeated the request, Baker would cheerfully kill him. Florence, ill again with malaria, launched into a tirade against the king in Arabic, none of which Kamrasi understood. He understood the body language, however, and more especially the gun's muzzle, and lessened the request to Baker's kilt and compass. He did not get either. 'I trust,' fumed Baker, 'I have seen the last of Kamrasi. A greater brute cannot exist.'

Next came the Bunyoro, whom Speke had assumed were the lost tribe of Israel. They were well dressed and highly musical, and Baker may have already regretted his frustrated comment of months earlier – 'There is neither gratitude, pity, love or self denial; no idea of duty; no religion, but covetousness, ingratitude, selfishness and cruelty.'[7] The Anti-Slavery Society might not like it and it would be heresy to make these observations today, but Baker was reporting what every European in Africa saw. Kamrasi warned the Bakers about travelling further. Some natives had told them the Lake of Dead Locusts was six months' travelling time away. Even Kamrasi's twenty days sounded like eternity. But this close to his goal, Samuel Baker would not be deterred. His escort from Kamrasi wore their battle gear – antelope horns, leopard- and monkey-skin cloaks and oxtails. They whooped and trilled and engaged in mock fights, warning off terrified villagers as they advanced. They also caroused into the early hours so that an early start before the sun was high was impossible. Baker called them the Devil's Own regiment. When an ox died in a swamp, the body was brought to Baker's tent. He offered the carcase to the men, but they were appalled. They never ate anything that died from natural causes. 'I must say nothing against these niggers after this,' Baker wrote. 'They are annoying but this covers many sins.'

Two weeks into the march and the expedition was on the point of collapse. The Bakers themselves grew weaker, Florence having to be carried constantly in an *angarep*, a litter. Only twelve Arabs remained. They were crossing a wide and dangerous swamp when Florence, on foot that day, suddenly stopped and sank into the morass. Her face was purple, her eyes rolling in her head. Somehow, Samuel got her to dry land and changed her wet clothes. He massaged her heart while the two slave women rubbed her feet. The Morning Star was dying. Baker dismissed his noisy escort, and by the next dawn they had slunk away. He rarely slept now, keeping a constant watch on Florence, grimly aware that he had been here before. 'F,' he wrote sadly, 'seems to have congestion of the brain . . . is so terrible a sacrifice to be the result of my selfish exile?'

They still travelled on, the comatose Florence in the litter. There was no food in the villages they reached. This was Buganda, and Mutesa's raiders had already taken everything. It was not until 4 March that Florence recovered. 'F woke up,' Baker wrote, 'from her delirium.' It had been a close call. She had regained consciousness in time to hear the men hacking at the hard ground with their mattocks. They were digging her grave.

Overjoyed at her recovery, Baker's heart fell again when the mist cleared to reveal the Ruwenzori mountain range, then known as the Mountains of the Moon. If the lake he sought was beyond them, then he knew that no one would survive that climb. The natives kept jabbering 'Parkani', which Baker took to mean the village name. In fact it meant, in Bugandan, 'Very close'. The next day, with Florence on her litter and Baker riding his last ox, they at last saw a sight that no white man had seen before.

'The glory of our prize burst suddenly upon me!' Baker wrote, 'There, like a sea of quicksilver, lay far beneath the grand expanse of water.' It took the suffering but delighted couple two hours to reach the shore. Florence tied green, white and red ribbons, the colours of her native Hungary, to a bush. Baker had planned to shout, 'Three cheers for old England,' but in the event he simply knelt on the pebbles at the water's edge and thanked his God. 'With a heart full of gratitude, I drank deeply from the sources of the Nile,' wrote Samuel White Baker.

Chapter 9

'Sacrifices to Geography'

On 24 February 1864 Francis Galton, secretary of the Royal Geographical Society, wrote to John Baker asking him if he knew of Samuel's specific whereabouts. John was a member of the society, and it had become urgent, perhaps for the society's very survival, that Baker the successful sportsman prove that he was also Baker the successful explorer. At that point, he was still three weeks away from the Lake of Dead Locusts, but John had no clue where he was.

Both Speke and Baker, brave and resourceful men though they were, made mistakes of geography. Far from the Dead Locust Lake being an inland sea, it was only 100 miles long and 20 miles wide. Its deepest point is 160 feet and the inhospitable scarp slopes that surround much of it made large settlements impossible. It is much smaller than Lake Victoria and less important in terms of the Nile's source, though very much part of the story of the Nile's course. Baker would realize in the years ahead that the unusual atmospheric conditions of the area gave an altogether false impression of the lake's size.

But all Baker's findings, his diary, his drawings and sketch maps, would be pointless unless he could get them home. The shrunken party, still ill with recurring malaria, and with Florence recovering from severe sunstroke, stayed at a little fishing village called Vacovia (the nearest English pronunciation). The lake crawled with crocodiles and the shores were a fever trap. There was a brief celebration of a roasted ox, and Baker made a rousing speech to try to lift everyone's spirits.

A week later the expedition had acquired two unwieldy dugout canoes and eight rowers. Baker made a canopy from bamboo and ox-hide as shelter for Florence, and later a sail from the plaid of his Atholl tartan. They had dried fish and live chickens on board. Baker had to hold himself in check with so many crocodiles and hippopotami wallowing in the waters around the boats; he would normally have taken this opportunity for some rough shooting. The rain turned the voyage into another grim struggle. The oarsmen were incompetent, and progress agonizingly slow. A sense of doom grew among the men. They believed themselves 'sacrifices to geography', as Baker wrote. Ball lightning terrified everybody – Baker was among the first Englishmen to witness it – and the sudden squalls for which the lake is notorious hit with a vengeance, confirming Baker's belief that this was a sea.

After nearly two weeks' sailing, the shoreline became matted with the same water hyacinths that characterized the sudd. Baker's altitude readings made no sense. From Speke's figures, he was 1,000 feet adrift, and despite a recurrence of Florence's malaria, it was a problem he had to solve. Gradually, they became aware of the lake narrowing to a river's width, and the roar they heard explained the Speke conundrum. The Bakers had found a magnificent waterfall, unknown to any white man, and despite the ramming of their boat by a bull hippopotamus, Baker's rowers steadied the vessel long enough for him to draw the falls in all their cascading magnificence.

There was no more to be done. 'I am so ill,' Baker scribbled in his diary, 'that I can hardly stand,' and, uncharacteristically for a man of action and decision, 'I do not know what to do.' He often could not walk and took castor oil baths in an effort to keep going, concerned all the time that Florence was worse than he was. There was little food available where they camped by the great falls, but they munched wild spinach and made tea from thyme. He was at his lowest ebb at this point, both of them utterly exhausted. They both contemplated death. 'There would be no more suffering,' the diary read, 'no fever; no long journey before us, that in our weak state was an infliction; the only wish was to lay down the burthen.'[1]

After two months, Baker sent a message to Kamrasi, whose aid he desperately needed. Bearing in mind the two had parted with Baker pointing a pistol at the king, it was good of him to send fifty men and litters to bring Baker to his camp. In fact, there was an ulterior motive. In a pantomime moment which only Africa could produce, it turned out that the man Baker assumed was Kamrasi was not the king, but his brother. The real Kamrasi needed Baker's skill and guns to help him wage war against a neighbouring tribe. Baker's presence turned out to be helpful. He would not fight personally, but organized a defence of the village and ran up the Union flag over it, with yet more dire warnings of the consequences if anyone harmed this 'protectorate'. They would all feel the wrath of the Great White Mother and her soldiers.

By Christmas 1864, nearly at Gondokoro, Baker had recovered his cheerful old self: 'No beef nor plum pudding and all those most dear far, far away, but ... my heart is light, my limbs are strong ... May I soon meet all those who will recognize my race being won.' Florence had unofficially adopted a 2-year-old slave boy, Abbai, whose mother had been flogged and sold. He slept under her chair in the evenings, and she washed him before putting him to sleep on his mat. Samuel handled the older boys, teaching them to shoot accurately with bows and arrows aimed at pumpkins. 'Poor little Abbai,' Baker wrote on 15 March, when they at last reached Gondokoro: 'I often wonder what will be his fate and whether in his dreams he recalls the few months of happiness that brightened his earliest days of slavery.'

The journey by river to Khartoum was horrendous. There was plague in the city. Whether this was the bubonic or pneumonic strain is not clear. There was no cure for either in the 1860s, and although plague had all but disappeared from western Europe, it remained a virulent problem in Africa. Reports reached the Bakers that half Khartoum's population was dead. Baker ordered the boat to be scrubbed with boiling water and sand, and fumigated it by burning tobacco. Two weeks later Saat, the faithful slave boy, fell victim to the disease. Florence bathed his face and moistened his dry mouth with sugar water. They buried him in a mimosa stand, not far from the grave of the expedition's first victim, Johann Schmidt.

Baker's diary ends at Khartoum. He was already writing up his notes into book form and he sent letters home. Robert Colquhoun, the consul-general in Alexandria, received news that Baker had named the Dead Locust Lake, Lake Albert, in honour of the recently departed prince consort, the idea which may have crossed Baker's mind from the moment he read of the man's death. To Roderick Murchison he wrote to tell him that the splendid waterfalls were to be named after him. Murchison was delighted. Baker wrote to his brothers and sisters, who were overjoyed to find him still alive after so long a silence.

It was not until 30 June that the Bakers left Khartoum, having survived the plague threat. They had caught up on old news – the disaster of the Dutch ladies, the fall from grace of John Petherick. The Bakers had seen enough of the Nile to last a lifetime, and crossed the desert now by camel to the Red Sea and then went by steamer to Suez. They got there in September, missing by a week the return of David Livingstone, who had a reputation to restore and a martyr's grave to find.

Gradually, at each stage of the journey, the primitive fell away and civilization closed in. The euphoria of this is best summed up by Baker himself, who found Allsopp's Pale Ale was on draught in an English hotel: 'What an Elysium! The beds had sheets and pillow-cases! ... I felt inclined to talk to everyone. Never was I so in love with my own countrymen and women ... had I really come from the Nile Sources? It was no dream.'[2]

To trek through hostile Africa and achieve what Baker had was one thing. But now he had to face hostility of a different and more personal kind. The first problem was that in his absence the Royal Geographical Society appeared to be on the point of committing collective suicide. The hysteria surrounding Speke's return had collapsed in the invective between him and Burton, to the extent that armchair geographers now doubted the claims of either man. Since Speke had gone to Africa with public funds from the royally backed Geographical Society, it looked as though the society itself might become a laughing stock.

Even David Livingstone, who at various times since the 1850s has been virtually canonized, was deemed to have let the society down. The expedition to the Zambezi, which Baker had tried to join, had cost the British taxpayer upwards of £50,000, and there was a large loss of life among the missionaries to malaria. The catch-all tag-line which made people feel better about the Zambezi expedition was 'commerce and Christianity'. Those who, like Baker himself, did not approve of the muscular conversion of natives could at least reflect that trade was being opened up to British advantage. In fact, neither was successful. Not unnaturally, black Africans were not impressed by the auburn-haired white man whom Dr Livingstone told them was the son of God when he showed them pictures of Jesus imagined by an English artist.

Commerce in Africa was proving an elusive white elephant. In 1902 the economic historian J.H. Clapham was wondering where it had all gone wrong. A mixture of native culture and inhospitable climates meant that Africa could never be developed along European lines. The work was too hard and – with the exception of Cecil Rhodes' Kimberley diamond mines – the profits too small. The newspapers slammed Livingstone, even pouring doubt on his claim to have found a cure for malaria, a mixture of rhubarb, jalap, calomel and quinine. It was perhaps unfortunate that Livingstone had publicly said that as a result malaria was 'not a whit more dangerous than the common cold'. Speke had tarnished his own reputation by a scathing attack on Petherick. He and Grant had spoken to Robert Colquhoun about him in Alexandria, and rumours were soon flying that Petherick was up to his eyes in the slave trade. Speke actually lied to the Geographical Society when he told them that he had left the Welshman 'in perfect health and excellent spirits'; in fact both he and his wife were seriously ill. The Foreign Office was soon involved. Lord John Russell, the foreign secretary, asked Speke if he knew of anyone who could go to Khartoum and suspend Petherick personally. One of the problems of running an empire in the days before modern communications was the length of time everything took. Telegrams might not arrive; letters were retained at hotels and embassies; so much was based on luck. Both Petherick and his wife wrote to *The Times*, at that period *the* mouthpiece of the great and good, explaining the reality of the situation. To the vast majority, who knew nothing about the difficulties of life in Africa, it fell on deaf ears.

If Speke was expecting a knighthood for his finds – and he clearly was – he went about it in a very odd way. He refused to submit a paper to the Geographical Society, which was the norm, in case it jeopardized sales of his forthcoming book. The *Journal of the Discovery of the Source of the Nile* was a huge tome at 650 pages, but Blackwood the publisher had to work very hard to tone down the libellous passages about Petherick and the various references to African sexual practices, for which he clearly thought the world was not ready. The timing was good, with huge Christmas sales at the end of 1864. Furious, Petherick's family launched a counter-attack against Speke, printing pamphlets privately and distributing them themselves.

When a number of important officials in Khartoum added their voices in support of Petherick, public opinion turned against Speke, as did Roderick Murchison of the Geographical Society. To cap it all, Speke was the toast of Paris in the spring of 1865, hobnobbing with the Empress Eugénie and planning another expedition with French backing. Murchison wrote to Grant, who wisely kept in the background throughout all this, moaning about Speke's 'wild and impracticable scheme of regimenting niggers and proselytizing Africa on a new plan'.

The upshot of all the internecine unpleasantness was tragic. Murchison invited Burton and Speke to take part in a debate on the sources of the Nile. In Murchison's mind, this might have been a sort of replay of the Huxley/Wilberforce debates in Oxford. It was unfortunate that both times that Speke had made his discoveries, his respective partners, Burton and Grant, had not been physically present to witness the event. Burton was a gifted linguist and a brilliant public speaker, whereas Speke hated giving public addresses and did so badly. His deafness did not help. Burton had been biding his time since the original quarrel, but he now produced his own book, *The Nile Basin*, in which his co-author, the octogenarian explorer and plantation owner James McQueen, spent pages talking about Speke's capers with African virgins, and positing the idea that Buranda would be full of people 'half black and half white'.

Speke might well have sued McQueen over this, but he never read the book. The day before the debate was to be held in Bath, he went partridge-shooting and was found dead in a field some hours later with shotgun wounds to the chest. Grant, Murchison and Livingstone were the only non-family members to attend his funeral. Among the papers found in Speke's study was an unfinished letter, dated 14 September 1864 – 'I have great fears about the fate of Baker.'

Honours were heaped on Samuel Baker even before he got home. On 22 May 1865 John received the Geographical Society's gold medal on his brother's behalf. Murchison's address praised Samuel's 'vigorous exploration, entirely at his own cost', his finding of Speke and Grant and 'his noble endeavour to complete the discoveries of those travellers'. Secretly, Murchison was delighted that Baker had gone alone – at least there would be no more bickering between exploring partners which had brought the society into such disrepute. Two others who received medals at the same time were Captain Montgomerie, who had carried out a survey from the Punjab into the heart of Mongolia, and Arminius Vambery, who had travelled throughout Asia 'in the guise and character of a Holy Dervish'. The eccentric Dr Vambery was an orientalist and linguist from Hungary who would, thirty years later, give vampire folklore information to his friend Bram Stoker for a book he was writing called *Dracula*.[3]

From Marseilles the Bakers caught trains to Paris. Samuel had sent a telegram to his youngest brother, James, to meet him there. James had first had a career in the navy, joining as a midshipman at the age of 15, then joined the 8th Hussars, as we have seen, and had taken a Cambridge degree in his thirties. He was now a staff officer and had a fascinating colonial career ahead of him. We do not know what James's reaction to Florence was, but the photograph taken in a Paris studio in October 1865 is, even by Victorian standards, odd. Smiles are rare in photographs of the time because of the length of exposure time, but the glum faces on all three are glummer than usual. This is the first known picture of Florence, and she is looking fashionably in Samuel's direction (the queen had several similar taken of her looking adoringly at Albert and even at his marble bust after his death) and is wearing a middle-Eastern outfit. She looks tanned and exotic. Samuel looks equally tanned and his blonde hair appears decidedly darker than it really was. He looks stern and troubled in all depictions of him. James looks a little embarrassed, like the gooseberry he possibly was, with an ill-fitting hat pulled down over his eyes.

After two weeks in Paris, where of course the pair were unknown, they sailed for Dover, James having gone ahead to make arrangements for a quick, discreet wedding. The couple stayed, as man and wife, at a lodging house in the Esplanade, and then caught a train to London. Here, of course, Samuel might be recognized, and they took a risk staying at Stephen Collins's lodging house in Arlington Street, Mayfair. They were to marry by special licence, which avoided the reading of banns in church, but did require a fifteen-day residence in the parish. It must have required careful handling because Baker's club, the Windham, was not far away, in St James's Square. On 24 October the first written inkling of the explorer's return came with an entry in the Windham's ledgers – 'Mr S.W. Baker has returned to England and paid his subscription.'

In some ways the timing of Baker's arrival and the days that led up to the wedding were fortuitous. Lord Palmerston, the 81-year-old prime minister, 'this terrible m'lord' who shouted at foreigners and put the fear of God and the British navy into them, died, and the funeral distracted the public: on 27 October, all London, it seemed, lined the streets to pay their last respects. James, now working at the War Office in Whitehall, lived near Arlington Street, and his wife, Louisa, and Florence became good friends virtually overnight.

For Samuel, the biggest problem would be to break the news about Florence to his four daughters. Ethel was 10 and probably had very few memories of her father, Constance was 12, Agnes was 14 and Edith, 18; all four had effectively been brought up by Baker's sister Min. She was in her early 30s by now, naturally regarded herself as the girls' mother rather than aunt, and found the necessary adjustment to Florence difficult. She wrote in the weeks that followed to her sister Ann:

> Of course, he ought to marry her [Florence] at once and we must receive her with kindness and affection ... but as to future arrangements, I feel there would be something to sadden all concerned ... my view of it is this, the children must know and love her, but Sam must not place her in a mother's position towards them.

She suggested two homes – one in London with Florence and the other in the country with Min and the girls.

Ann was the wife of a squire in Worcestershire by this time, and Baker went to see her to break the news about Florence. He wrote to Edith, but still did not see 'his chicks' just yet. The wedding took place at St James's, Piccadilly, on Saturday 4 November. The Reverend John Oakley officiated, and the only witnesses were James and Louisa. Having posed as Mrs Baker for so long, Florence almost wrote that name in the ledger, but altered it in time to 'Florence B.

Finnian', with an English spelling. That evening, the genuinely married Mr and Mrs Baker dined with Roderick Murchison, who was desperately looking for a hero who would restore the reputation of his society. Even as they dined, the artist Thomas Baines was at work on the preliminary sketches for his oil painting of the Murchison Falls. The canvas was 8 feet high.

The septuagenarian Murchison was very much taken with Florence: 'His little blue-eyed Hungarian wife,' he wrote in a subsequent letter, 'who he picked up when abroad has accompanied him during all his five years in Africa and is still only 23 years of age ... We all like her very much.' The following week, Baker gave a lecture on his expedition to the Geographical Society in Burlington House. It was a huge success, especially as the *Morning Herald* reported Baker's age as 'a little over thirty', whereas in fact he was 44 by now. Florence was included in the lecture, curtseying graciously in front of the (largely male) audience, and received a standing ovation for the trials and tribulations she had endured at her husband's side.

Behind the scenes of course the Victorian hypocrisy/rumour mill was working overtime. Even the saintly Livingstone had a comment to make. In a letter to William Oswell in January of the following year he wrote: 'Baker married his mistress at Cairo and from all accounts she deserved it after going through all she did for him. I heard about his woman, but it was not made public and if she turns out well, better it never should be.' Christopher Rigby, who had been consul in Zanzibar, wrote to Grant about 'the Wallachian lady', and wrote shrewishly that he 'could not understand what Mrs Baker he referred to'.

Grant in fact was quietly seething at Baker's lionization and this grew worse once his book was published. *The Albert N'yanza: Great Basin of the Nile* was a reworking of Baker's African diary. His publisher, sure of another Baker hit, offered an astonishing £4,500 advance and a 50 per cent royalty payment, or £2,500 and 66 per cent royalties. Baker took the latter. In February 1866 he was elected to the hugely prestigious Athenaeum Club, along with the pre-Raphaelite painter John Millais. The Bakers moved to a suite of rooms in Alwood's Hotel in Savile Row and then a house overlooking Regent's Park.

By the end of May, the book appeared in two volumes and the reviews were excellent. The influential *Quarterly Review* said: 'The best parts of the English character have rarely been more admirably exemplified than by Mr Baker in his manifold trials, perplexities and privations.' The *Daily News* reported that Florence was 'a refined English lady'. William Gladstone, leader of the Liberal opposition, believed the end of the book was a masterpiece (although to be fair, Gladstone's own writing was incredibly turgid). Lord Stanley, son of the prime minister, the Earl of Derby, wrote to his father and to Benjamin Disraeli, chancellor of the Exchequer: 'Baker is a man of some private fortune and I am told he does not want money. I would knight him.' And in August 1866, Mr Baker became Sir Samuel, the first family member to receive a knighthood in 300 years.

Grant was outraged. Since his family already had a coat of arms (the Grants were an ancient Scottish noble family) he was granted by the College of Arms a new set of supporters for his shield – African animals. He wrote to Blackwood, the publisher, 'By God! I have never heard of anything more disgusting to us' (himself and Speke), and claimed, ludicrously, that Florence had been a barmaid in a European town when Baker met her. In the event, Grant had to make do with becoming a CB (Commander of the Bath) and was advised to keep quiet. With the exception of the Bakers – and of course, in Victorian society, they would not have been regarded as an exception – nobody emerges with honour from Africa.

The success of the *Albert N'yanza* book prompted Baker and his publisher to follow it up with *The Nile Tributaries of Abyssinia and the Sword Hunters of the Hamran Arabs*, which Macmillan produced in the autumn of 1867. It ran to eight editions up to 1894, and most reviewers preferred it to the *Albert N'yanza*. The Bakers were invited to Paris by the French Geographical Society and again got a standing ovation when Baker gave the medal he had just been awarded to Florence. Perhaps it was the meeting up again with Guillaume Lejean that turned Baker into a sudden Francophile. The 'vermin' had long ago turned into the 'ami', and Baker made suitable *entente cordiale* noises throughout his stay. The Parisian journal *Le Tour du Monde* serialized Baker's books and threw in a lot of African nudity for good measure. Since Paris was accepted by many – and with good reason – as the centre of European pornography, no one was too surprised.

In that autumn the Bakers took out a lease on Hedenham Hall, a manor house in Norfolk. The vicar here, Robert Marshall, was now Edith's husband, and Florence had thrown herself into the wedding arrangements in the full role of mother, which cannot have pleased Min very much. So many guests were invited that the Bakers had to add a conservatory to house them. It was in this period that Baker produced his only novel – *Cast up by the Sea* – a rattling yarn for boys which did well. It was autobiographical in that the hero saves a man from drowning and the heroine, Polly, can be identified with Florence. It ran to ten editions in Baker's lifetime and a posthumous eleventh as late as 1931.

Baker's new family life was one thing. Fame – he already had a relative fortune – was another. But with all this, there was something missing in Samuel Baker's life – adventure. 'England is too tame,' he wrote in more than one letter, and longed for Africa again. There were two causes célèbres which may have provided opportunities. One was the apparent disappearance of David Livingstone. He wrote to Murchison: 'I would be delighted to go and meet my old friend Livingstone, if he lives. The inactivity of my present life is worse than an African fever.' In the event, it was the Welsh journalist Henry Stanley who 'found' Livingstone (although of course he was never actually lost) and provided one of the most famous journalistic tag-lines of the nineteenth century.

The other opportunity was the high-handed behaviour of Theodore, Emperor of Abyssinia, who had captured a missionary party. Baker wrote to Lord Wharncliffe that if he and his brother Valentine were allowed to strike at Theodore through the country of 'my old friend Mek Nimmur' with two squadrons of the 10th Hussars, all would be well. 'I am vain enough to think that in a few months I would either have Theodore as a living exhibition in the Zoological gardens – or stuffed in a glass case at the British Museum.'

But this kind of lightning commando raid was not the British way – it was left to the Boers in 1899 to show them how. Instead, 40,000 men under General Robert Napier were sent to do the job. It worked, but was slow and hideously expensive (£9 million in today's terms). Bearing in mind the fact that Napier at one point faced an army 12,000 strong, the Baker boys' two squadrons would have been swallowed whole.

The actual way forward for Samuel was via the Prince of Wales. 'Bertie' had been married for four years by this time, but his mother still shadowed his every move. She would nevertheless rather not know what her wayward eldest got up to at various country-house shooting weekends. One of these was at Dunrobin, the enormous Scottish home of the Duke of Sutherland, and the Bakers were there too. Bertie had a hankering to visit Egypt and asked Baker to accompany him. There was no provision made for Lady Baker – the only time until the end of his life that they were separated – but this was an opportunity the African explorer could not pass up. He spoke fluent Arabic and knew Egypt and the Nile so well, he was the obvious choice for guide. The plan was to visit Ismail Pasha, the Khedive of Egypt, and sail up the river as far as the second cataract, shooting crocodile as they went.

On 9 February 1869 the prince wrote to his mother: 'We find Sir Samuel Baker very agreeable and with so much to tell me about the country, which no one knows better than he does – that I cannot say how glad I am to have him accompany me here.'

The Nile party, accompanied by William Howard Russell, *The Times* correspondent who had covered the Crimean War, enjoyed themselves immensely. When the 1,200-mile round trip was over, there was a series of balls and parties held in Cairo and Alexandria. At one masked ball, the khedive took the Prince of Wales and the African explorer aside. He had a proposal for Samuel White Baker.

Chapter 10

Baker Pasha

'My country,' said Ismail Pasha in 1879, 'is no longer in Africa; we are now a part of Europe. It is therefore natural for us to abandon our former ways and to adopt a new system adapted to our social conditions.' For Egypt to become European, Ismail required help. And that, in part, came from Samuel Baker. Official portraits of Ismail the Magnificent show a solid-looking man with a full beard, rather less grand than Baker's, and a glittering array of largely self-awarded orders on his French frock coat. The only thing that marks him out as Egyptian is his scarlet fez, which all officials of the government wore.

Ismail was actually Albanian, as were many generals and diplomats of the ailing Ottoman empire, and he was nine years younger than Samuel Baker. He had been educated in Paris and spent his young manhood as emissary on behalf of his uncle Said, Wali of Egypt and the Sudan. In this context, he had wide experience of the Vatican, the French court of Napoleon III and the Porte, the Ottoman government of Constantinople. When Said died early in 1863, Ismail inherited the title, although styled himself khedive, a higher title which the Porte at first refused to sanction in that it gave the man more status than they cared to bestow. By 1873, however, when the Bakers left Africa forever, Egypt and its ruler were virtually independent from the Porte.

Ismail launched into a series of European-style reforms from 1863 onwards, reorganizing the post office and the customs service, sponsoring commerce, building palaces, establishing a sugar industry and remodelling sections of Cairo after the style of Paris. A huge railway network was launched on the British pattern, and under Ismail's khedivate the Suez Canal Company set about transforming global trade. In this context, Ismail courted the attention of both

Britain and France, as the foremost technological powers in Europe, and his vast personal charm was brought into play when he visited London and Paris in 1867 and again in 1869. It was a mark of the esteem in which he was held that Victoria herself welcomed him – in the late 1860s she was still in deepest mourning for Albert, and kept her official engagements to an infuriating minimum. During the second visit Ismail watched a review of the fleet at Spithead and realized, if he did not know it already, the awesome power of the British navy.

In terms of internal politics, Ismail established in November 1866 an assembly of delegates. Probably intended as an advisory body, the delegates assumed more power as the years passed. It could never be called a parliament in the British sense, but it was also a far cry from the days of the absolute power of Eastern potentates, and by the mid-1870s the delegates were strong enough to pressure Ismail to change various laws in their favour.

It was perhaps his awareness of the size of the British empire that pointed the khedive south into the Sudan and east to the Red Sea. The northern stretches of the totemic Nile were his already, but he wanted to control the southern reaches and the river's source, the area recently put on the map by Baker. This was the background to the extraordinary offer made by the khedive. Samuel Baker would become Baker Pasha, the first Briton to be granted that Ottoman title. He would become governor-general of the Equatorial Nile Basin, on a salary of £10,000 a year to run for four years. He would have an army of 1,645 men, a mixed force of infantry, irregular cavalry and artillery. And his main brief was to suppress the slave trade.

The jury is still out on the motives of Ismail Pasha. His reforms were ruinously expensive. The handsome salary given to Baker was a drop in the ocean. The khedive spent an estimated £5 million on his harem, and it was patently obvious that a poor, essentially agricultural country such as Egypt could not possibly repay the huge debts owed to Europe. Dorothy Middleton has no doubts about Ismail – 'this fat tyrant with his drooping eyelid, his household of slaves and his ever-open purse' – but contemporaries as different from each other as Baker and his successor, Charles Gordon, believed in him implicitly. The British Anti-Slavery Society was not impressed. If the khedive really wanted to stamp out slavery in his domains, why not start by freeing them in his own household? The whole venture smacked of cynicism. Ismail merely wanted to extend his realm by annexing the Sudan, believed the society, and it was disgraceful that an Englishman should be used as a pawn in this dubious enterprise.

It is possible to see Baker as the leader of a crusade against slavery in the Livingstone or Wilberforce mould. 'May Heaven's rich blessing,' Livingstone had written, 'come down on any one, American, English, Turk, who will help to heal this open sore of the world.' Baker was not an evangelist – we have seen already his views on missionaries – and when he was a child, of course, his own family still owned slaves. But he had seen first hand the horrors of the African slave trade, the burnt and deserted villages, the flogged and raped women, the slave-ships carrying smallpox and other deadly infections along with their human cargoes.

But Baker, with his public-school values and British sense of justice, was also a realist, as anyone was who had spent time in Africa. The Anti-Slavery Society was hopelessly naive. Having abandoned slavery in the empire in 1833, the government, typically, sought to impose its views on the rest of the world. In 1839 the British navy high-handedly stopped and searched Portuguese ships suspected of carrying slaves, and most of the country looked on appalled at the barbarism of the southern states of America that clung to the indefensible. The argument the pro-slavery lobby put forward there applied even more in the East and in Africa: slavery was an essential part of the fabric of society. To remove it would be to create, as Baker said, 'a carriage without wheels'. In a lecture he gave at Cambridge in 1874 he made his views plain, and no doubt they shook some of the liberals listening to him. The abolition of 1833 he said was 'chivalrous' but 'foolish'. Thousands of people with no education or skills suddenly found themselves free (as they would thirty years later in the United States), and they did not know how to cope. 'The negro,' he wrote:

has been, and still is, thoroughly misunderstood. However severely we may condemn the horrible system of slavery, the results of emancipation have proved that the negro does not appreciate the blessings of freedom, nor does he show the slightest feeling of gratitude to the hand that broke the rivets of his fetters ... he was suddenly freed and from that moment refused to work and instead of being a useful member of society, he not only became a useless burden to the community, but a plotter and intriguer, imbued with a deadly hatred to the white man who had generously declared him free.[1]

Liberals then and now would point out that it was the white man (and the Arabs) who had put the fetters there in the first place, but Baker's solution was gradual emancipation and strong, paternal government. It was not unlike the 'Tory Democracy' being advocated by Disraeli around this time for the future of the working class in Britain, hopelessly patronizing as the idea is by today's standards.

And if any man could free the slaves and provide paternal government in the Sudan, it was Baker Pasha. He wrote to his friend Wharncliffe in more detail in the late spring of 1869. The first priority was to suppress slavery, then came the annexation of the Nile Basin. This involved the establishment of peace between various warring tribes that Baker had met before. In doing this, as in ending slavery, he would be effectively changing a system that was centuries old. The paternalist government that he and the khedive envisaged was to establish cotton production as the heart of the economy in exchange for 'Manchester goods'. He was to open permanent navigation between the Albert and Victoria N'yanza and to establish a series of trading posts in the area. Each local tribe was to cultivate a certain amount of corn in addition to cotton and ivory; flax and beeswax were also exchangeable commodities.

There is a huge gulf between the *notion* of empire – the technologically advanced, morally superior British lording it over the natives – and the reality. On the face of it, Baker had absolute authority under the khedive; and since the khedive would be far to the north and often unreachable in Cairo, that in effect made Baker the sole power in the Sudan. The practicalities – and Baker, the brilliant organizer, was pre-eminently a practical man – were somewhat different.

His staff was only fifteen strong, excluding the unpaid Florence, who often did the work of ten men in the months ahead. His ADC was Lieutenant Julian Baker, his nephew, seconded from the Royal

Navy at a salary from the khedive of £500 a year. The man, like all the Bakers, was easy-going and highly competent. Edwin Higginbottom, who would not survive Baker's tenure, was chief engineer over a small team who would handle the various Nile navigational structures. James McWilliam was the engineer in charge of the Nile steamers. Michael Marcopolo was both interpreter and stockkeeper. Dr Joseph Gedge was the medical officer – he would not survive either.

Baker's army of 1,645 was not the fine body of men he might have hoped for. In fact the military success of the Egyptian army, unless stiffened by the British, was not impressive for the rest of the century. The 250-strong cavalry unit was '*very* irregular' according to Baker, and he dismissed them after the first review as being next to useless. One of his two infantry regiments was made up mostly of Egyptian convicts who would prove unreliable under fire and drift away at the earliest opportunity. Baker was more hopeful of the other unit, the Sudanese, who had seen action and were far more dependable in a crisis. It was from these ranks that he recruited his famous Forty Thieves (actually forty-six) under the command of Lieutenant Colonel Abd-el-Kader. The loyalty of these men was extraordinary; Abd-el-Kader earned the nickname of 'the Englishman' as a result.

Because of the inevitable transport difficulties, Baker's expedition converged on Khartoum by three different routes. Two sailed up the Nile, with Baker bringing up the rear, and the third went overland under Higginbottom, carrying the prefabricated sections of steamers with a vast camel caravan, 1,000 strong. A combination of the river levels and the usual Egyptian delaying tactics (not everyone in the khedive's country accepted his reforms) meant that the start was late. The fifteen sloops and fifteen *diahbiahs* with their sails coped well, but the steamers were held back by the cataracts and it would be months before Baker could use them.

Baker's arrival at Khartoum did not go down well. No doubt he wore his elaborate frock coat as pasha and carried the Mameluke sabre of a general of the Ottoman army. The governor-general, Djaffer Pasha, whom Baker had met at Suakin the last time he was in Africa, perhaps felt threatened, and the new pasha realized at once the cross-purposes involved in the expedition. Djaffer had just sent the slaver Kutchuck Ali with eleven boats to form an outpost on the frontier. This was in effect a slave-taking enterprise: Djaffer was sanctioning the very thing that Baker was supposed to be stamping out. Perhaps it was only now that the sheer size of his task dawned on Baker. He was master of half a million square miles of Africa (no one in Britain other than the queen could claim that) but he would face opposition to his rule at every level and every turn. Ironically, had Baker ignored the clause in his contract about ending slavery, he would have received every help along the way and succeeded in every other respect.

Florence's journal, written in English, reflects the boundless optimism that she always shared with her husband. 'Thank God we are at last off,' she wrote on 8 February 1870, 'like a fleet going to war.'[2] The fleet would establish bases between Gondokoro and the Albert N'yanza and perhaps even find the still missing Livingstone in the process.

It was immediately obvious the effect that slavery and Ismail's increased taxation had had on the area. In *Ismailia*, the book that Baker wrote about this phase of his life, he paints a grim picture: 'The night, formerly discordant with the creaking of countless water-wheels, was now silent as death. There was not a dog to howl for a lost master.'[3] Wherever the expedition encountered slaves, Baker liberated them. The mudir (governor) of Fashoda was up to his neck in the trade. Both Florence and Julian wrote in their journals what a depressing place Fashoda was – 'full of fever' and 'the most miserable place that can be imagined'. Baker quizzed two locals who were brought on board the *diahbiah* that served as his float-ing headquarters. They told him that the governor regularly shot people, 'that he killed them like grass,' as Florence wrote, 'that they could not count how many were lying dead'. She was particularly horrified by the stories of the slave girls as the engineers smashed off their iron shackles – 'I am sure nobody could imagine,' wrote the ex-slave, 'what goes on in some parts of the world.'

But it was not far south of Fashoda that the sudd began to make progress impossible. The Nile was abnormally high and the vegeta-tion unusually thick. The boats had to be hauled and poled while the engineers tried to find flowing water. For two months this went on, the mosquitoes unbearable, the whole area alive with snakes and crocodiles. At night the snorting of the hippopotami kept everybody awake. What was so dispiriting about this journey was that as soon as a channel was found, the wind got up and within an hour the route was closed again by thick vegetation. Baker ordered channels to be cut, time and again, the men up to their waists in the 'frightful, stinking morass', hacking at the choking vegetation with swords, axes and bayonets. When one man died of sunstroke, there was no firm ground to bury him in. Baker noted ruefully in his diary 'the spirit of God apparently had not yet moved upon the waters', and when they came across a large crocodile, the men took out their frustration on the animal and hacked it to death, enjoying the meat later. The beast had not, Baker observed with his customary black humour, 'exactly fallen into the hands of the Royal Humane Society'. By the end of March, six men had died and there were 150 sick. Baker's imperial army was diminishing daily.

They made a camp at Sobat, which they called Tewfikyeh, in honour of Ismail Pasha's son Tewfik, and waited for slave-ships to arrive. Technically, Baker's writ carried no weight in the area. This was the country of the Shilluk tribe, outside the khedive's territory, but it is a good example of how Britain, mile by mile and even yard by yard, extended control. Kutchuck Ali meekly handed over 150 slaves on one occasion. Baker ordered a general wash of the liberated captives and for clothes to be provided for the naked women. He also gave orders that if any of the females wanted to marry one of his soldiers, that could be arranged. Such mass weddings were common in Africa, although it was the sort of thing that caused shudders back home in England. In an unusual snapshot of overt racism, Baker wrote: 'the black ladies had a strong antipathy to brown men [the Egyptian troops] and only chose Sudanese husbands. I saw the loving couples standing hand in hand. Some of the girls were pretty and my black troops had shown good taste in their selection.' The feistiness of the ex-slaves amused Baker, who wrote of their assertion of women's rights at a time when very few British women were demanding them.

The pasha established good relations with the Shilluk under their king, Quat Kare. His troops were told to behave themselves around the natives. On one occasion Baker had a thief brought in front of a firing squad and spared him at the last minute. It won hearts and minds. While Florence adopted a number of children and taught them gardening skills by growing melons, pumpkins, tomatoes, parsley, lettuce, beetroot and celery, Baker became very fond of some of his Forty, equipped them with modern Snider rifles and decked them out in blue tunics with red facings above Zouave-style baggy trousers and white puttees. Quat Kare and his many wives were regular visitors, cadging presents and being literally shocked by a magnetic battery that Higginbottom set up to amuse the natives.

Baker's return to Khartoum for supplies brought him news of the outside world. In Europe, war raged between France and Prussia, and Britain had been wise enough to keep out of it. A realist would have known the inevitable outcome. Wars had always been won by the side that got to best fighting ground first. In 1870 that meant the use of railways: the French had one line to the disputed area of Alsace-Lorraine – the Prussians, twenty-six. It was here too that Baker learned that his province was leased by the khedive to Agad & Co., ostensibly an ivory-trading business. But everyone knew that Agad was a slaver. The pasha still chose to believe in Ismail's sincerity and determined that when Agad's ivory contract ended in April 1872, he, on behalf of the government, would take it over then.

In the meantime, Ahmet Agad's son-in-law, Abou Saood, was, in European parlance, the managing director of the company, and Baker detested him. He was a crawling, fawning sycophant, with a shifty appearance, and a liar to his fingernails. It was Baker's greatest regret in later years that he hadn't had the man shot out of hand.

Julian Baker was ill with fever and Samuel had a cold. Dr Gedge died that autumn, but it was time to start south again. The station at Tewfikyeh was dismantled and loaded onto the boats. The men were dispirited. The sudd was as bad as ever, and the fast of Ramadan meant that the troops and boat-handlers were weaker than ever with hunger. While Abd-el-Kader and the Forty remained as loyal and efficient as ever, others were less so. Tayib Agha was always late or caught unawares, or not quite sure what was going on. Raouf Bey was bone idle and ignored orders when he could. The boats had to be loaded and unloaded continually to get through the sudd, and it was not until the middle of March that they reached clear water. The troops were ecstatic, shouting 'El hamd el Illah!' ('Thank God').

Three weeks later they were at Gondokoro. To the south-east, in the lands of the Shuli tribe, lay the most prominent slave-trading centres of Fatiko, Foweira, Fabko and Faloro. The Bari and Loquia tribes were fighting each other, as well as throwing in their lot with various slavers, almost as the wind changed direction. The task ahead was huge, but Baker took one day at a time. On 26 May 1871 Gondokoro was officially annexed on behalf of the khedive. It was an impressive occasion and it was designed to be. It was Baker's way of showing the tribal chieftains and the slavers that law and civilization had reached the Sudan. With Julian in his full dress naval uniform, his officers mounted and wearing theirs, Baker assembled his 1,200 remaining troops in their best uniforms and full pack, forming three sides of a hollow square. The fourth side was made up of ten field pieces which thundered out a cannonade as Baker read out the official annexation proclamation and ran up the star and crescent of the Ottoman government. There was a march past and much music from the band before a huge feast was laid on. Baker entertained his officers on the deck of his *diahbiah* with roast beef and even tinned plum duff which had not been eaten the previous Christmas. Julian put on a magic lantern show and had to repeat the process several times, so taken were the Muslims with the Red Sea parting for Moses.

In some ways, trouble was inevitable. Baker had come un-announced and unwelcome into alien territory. He was no longer an explorer in hunting gear with maps and a handful of bearers. He was the official representative of a distant and hated government, backed by armed forces. Towards the end of July, Raouf Bey's night sentries were literally caught napping by the first of several attacks from the natives. Luckily, Baker's own bodyguard, the ten men who formed the cream of the Forty, were fully alert and disaster was averted.

Baker carried out reprisals, leading a series of raids into the neighbouring territory. He had met the Bari before and knew their reputation. Julian was new to it all – 'The treachery of these niggers is beyond belief,' he wrote in his journal. The raids brought back freed slaves, corn and cattle, and there were even skirmishes fought along the riverbank in full view of Florence on the deck of the *diahbiah*.

Lieutenant Colonel Mike Snook in a recent article[4] makes the point that this period is a sort of limbo between the amateur wars ending with the Crimea in the 1850s and the first modern war against the Boers in 1899. Baker had artillery with him but no cavalry and no Maxim or Krupp guns, and he was always outnumbered in his clashes with natives. It would be nearly thirty years, at Omdurman on the Nile, before British technology and killing power could completely destroy a native army.

With a temporary and uncertain peace established, Baker officially renamed Gondokoro Ismailia, after the khedive, and began planting gardens again. Florence handled all the domestic arrangements with her usual sangfroid, supervising the now middle-aged Karka, who had accompanied the Bakers on their Albert N'yanza expedition, and a team of uniformed boys and girls. She found the boys much more capable and full of spirit than the girls, who were universally downtrodden and frequently lazy.

By the end of 1871, Baker was down to only 502 officers and men out of his original 1,645. He had his engineers, 52 sailors and about 300 camp followers, women and children. He had very few horses, plenty of corn and just over a year to go until his contract ended. Some men would have given up. On 22 January 1872 Raouf Bey was left in charge at Ismailia, and 212 officers and men marched south. They were led by the governor-general of the Equatorial Nile Basin, Samuel White Baker.

Chapter 11

Dancing with Baker

When he set out from Ismailia in early 1872, Baker had not received confirmation from the khedive that his governor-generalship had been extended by a year. In a sense this was irrelevant. There was a job to do. He had the engineers with him, 2,500 cattle and 1,800 sheep, as well as the prefabricated sections of a steamer. Since the porters promised by the ever-treacherous Bari were not forthcoming, even the Forty were drafted in to haul the carts. Baker sent the steamer sections back to Ismailia with orders to construct No. 2 boat. This could cut a channel through to Khartoum and keep that vital link open before the creeping sudd could close behind it.

At Affudo the expedition intended to set up a post near Miani's Tree, which they called Ibramiyeh. In the event this never happened, but Baker's successor, Gordon, followed the same plan three years later.

Baker's first objective was to set up camp at Fatiko, liberate slaves and add the best of them to his troops. There were 600 irregulars with Abou Saood, and Baker's plan was to dragoon them into government service. Commanders throughout history had done this, defeating an enemy and 'turning' them into loyal supporters. The problem for Baker was that his raw material was not very promising.

In respect of the Forty, however, he proved that it could be done. These men would have been able to hold their own on any battlefield in Europe and they put the fear of Allah into the slavers and tribesmen they faced. Lieutenant Colonel Abd-el-Kader was steady as a rock, and so was Captain Mohammed Deii. Corporal Monsoor was a Coptic Christian from Egypt and was a tower of strength. He never fell ill, could swim and dive like an otter and regarded himself as Baker's personal bodyguard. Major Abdullah had served in

117

Mexico under the French Marshal Bezaine in the brief interlude when Maximilian had been emperor there.

Baker had his Forty. The 'thieves' was a private cultural joke shared only among the Europeans of the expedition. Ironically, these were the men least likely to steal, and they would have been mortified to think that Baker might have believed them capable of it. Florence had her children. Amarn was the brightest of the freed slaves. Saat (named after the boy who died on the previous expedition) was strong and loyal. Bellal was quick to learn, but he was 14, of what Florence calls 'a rather savage disposition', and would probably rather not have been a servant to a woman. Florence's favourite was Kinyon, which meant crocodile, a handsome Bari who volunteered for service with the Bakers. Jarvah was the 'fat boy', a cook's mate who was inevitably the butt of a few jokes. The cook was Abdullah, excellent in the kitchen but poor at Arabic. The smallest and youngest was 6-year-old Cuckoo. They all wore a variant of the blue, red-faced jackets of the Forty and, as on the last expedition, Baker encouraged the lads in drill and spear-throwing when they had finished their duties. They could occasionally be cajoled into dancing with the girls by moonlight. Florence has less to say about the girls, as we have seen, but she does single out Fad-el-Kereem, who needed 'particular management owing to her strong passions, either for love or war'.[1]

They lost one of the Forty, Ali Nedjar, who drowned even before Baker sent the steamer sections back, and the Laboré natives, acting as porters in place of the missing Bari, were less than efficient. A whole case of brandy trickled out of its packaging when one of them carried it upside down for days. But a little of the comfort that Florence had assumed would be the norm as the governor-general's wife was obtained. Baker's journal talks of quiet evenings after dinner, smoking a pipe and listening to Julian's navy stories. There was occasional good shooting and the Europeans were much amused by the clown-like antics of their guide, Lokko, the rain-maker. Lokko was not anxious to mix it with the tribes around Fatiko, which the expedition reached in early March. Baker tied the man back to back with the son of the Laboré chief and let it be known they would both be shot if any of the porters deserted. This was familiar territory to the Bakers, who had passed this way before, and the explorer of elephant gun and Bowie knife was never far below the glittering uniform of the governor-general.

They marched into Fatiko in impressive array, all three Bakers on horseback at the head of the column, Colonel Abd-el-Kader and the Forty (by now reduced by three) and the rest of the troops. Four hundred porters carried the baggage, little Cuckoo with Baker's portmanteau on his head. The drums and bugles of the column heralded their arrival, and Baker watched through his telescope as the slavers in Fatiko hurried their contraband out of sight and the Bari assumed a battle formation. The emissaries were sent out to the column and as soon as they recognized Baker, they relaxed. With the slavers was Mahomet, the dragoman from their first Nile expedition. 'Ah, Mahomet,' Florence said when she saw him, 'I am very glad to see you; but how wretched you appear.' Completely overcome, the man dropped to his knees, kissed Florence's hand and burst into tears.

The Bakers quickly established a camp and got the regimental band playing. 'The natives,' wrote Baker, 'are passionately fond of music and I believe the safest way to travel in these wild countries would be to play the cornet, if possible, without ceasing, which would ensure a safe passage.'[2] He wore his full dress uniform, Julian his naval version, Florence a white crinoline, at the ball they held. 'Several old Venuses,' Baker wrote drily, 'were making themselves extremely ridiculous, as they sometimes do in civilized countries when attempting the allurements of younger days.'[3]

When the festivities were over, Baker got down to business. Locals told him of the depredations of the slavers, who of course merely travelled further afield in the face of a government clampdown. He was particularly interested to learn that not a single tusk of ivory had been transported by Agad & Co. (their official *raison d'être*) and that the leading slaver in the area was Mohamed Wat-el-Mek, with whom Baker had clashed before. The governor-general could do business with him.

Leaving a garrison of 100 at Fatiko, Baker set off on 18 March for Unyoro. The Shuli tribe were kept sweet by Baker supplying their sheikh, Rot Jarma, with a galaxy of trinkets including razors, a comb, earrings, mirrors and so on, and of course giving him a few jolts with Higginbottom's magnetic battery. In five days they reached Foweira, a dismal place of rain and potatoes, according to Baker, where the brutal slaver Suleiman held power. A civil war had just ended and the king Baker had known, Kamrasi, was dead, replaced by his son Kabba Rega. Suleiman signed on to the government service and promised to provide sixty-one men and to accompany Baker to his next objective, Masindi, Kabba Rega's kraal.

It all sounded too good to be true, and was. Suleiman delayed his start, and when Baker sent men back to see where he was, he discovered that Suleiman had killed a man in his care and his entire force had run to Fabko. He and his vakeel[4] Eddrees were dragged to Baker by the Forty, and faced a drumhead court martial. They were charged with murder, treason, conspiracy and insubordination, and both were found guilty. This arbitrary justice would be criticized when it reached the British press, but in fact in every European court the crimes of treason and murder were punished by death. Suleiman received 200 lashes instead – which was not much more of a punishment than that meted out to British soldiers guilty of far less serious crimes. The man had previously and personally cut off the buttocks of a boy with a hippopotamus hide whip, and nobody except Suleiman shed any tears at his punishment.

On 25 April the expedition reached Masindi and found Kabba Rega as intractable and unpleasant as his father. He wanted Baker's guns to use against his old enemy King Rionga, and he wanted presents. Everything else was irrelevant. The Bakers spent two months here, building a government house, clearing the long grass and growing a garden. The tribesmen called Baker Malaggé – the man with a beard – and he received an ambassador from King M'tesa of Uganda. He spent as much time with Kabba Rega as he could stand, if only to reassure his people he did not actually have three heads with six eyes each, as Abou Saood had apparently told them.

In *Ismailia* Baker describes proudly the government house. In keeping with Ottoman tradition, the main room was the divan, where the governor-general entertained his visitors. In practice there was not much more to it than a small passageway which led to the private quarters. The divan was a psychological tour de force, designed, like the Forty on parade, to impress and overawe. Scarlet blankets lined the cane-built walls, and carpets covered the floor. Mirrors threw reflections and light in all directions, and there were life-size portraits of the queen and the princess of Wales decorated with tinsel. There were also hunting scenes and rather gloomy oils of Highland landscapes, territory which might as well have been on the moon as far as Kabba Rega was concerned. Baker's guns, assiduously cleaned and oiled, stood in a large rack of their own, and the king and his chiefs stood in the centre of it all, covering their mouths in astonishment and occasionally whispering 'Wah! Wah!' when they were lost for words. On display too were the trinkets Baker used to exchange for ivory – Manchester cloth, scissors, clocks, whistles, triangles, tambourines, pop-guns and beads, things that any middle-class child at home took for granted, but which were tokens of wonderment for Africans.

Unyoro officially became Egyptian on 14 May, but at Fatiko, Abou Saood was once again raiding for slaves. It was the human version of the sudd. Wherever Baker himself went, there was progress, but as soon as his back was turned, the old ways closed in again. His attempts to secure free trade in ivory met with resistance. Anyone other than Kabba Rega found trading tusks with Baker would be killed, the king told his people. Baker's troops acted as police in the area. 'They were almost as good as London police,' he wrote: 'there were no areas to the houses, neither insinuating cooks or housemaids, nor even nursemaids with babies in perambulators, to distract their attention from their municipal duties.' The governor-general set up a school at Masindi, where the clerk Ramadan was teacher and a chief's son, Cherri-Merri, was a pupil.

But there was a tension building in this apparent calm. In mid-May there had been a rattle of war-drums in the night, horns and whistles being blown. Expecting an attack, Baker and Julian turned out the troops but at dawn there was no one to be seen. By the end of the month, it was noticeable that there were fewer women in the kraal each day. While Florence wrote casually of wanting to sail on the lake in an atmosphere of tranquillity, she must have known this would never happen. Kabba Rega was only 18 or 19 and not much of a warrior, but he was probably acting under the influence of Abou Saood when he launched an attack on the last day of the month.

Abd-el-Kader was drilling his men, so in that respect Kabba Rega's timing was bad. The sound of the drums brought nearly 5,000 warriors at the run, facing down Baker's tiny command. In essence it was not unlike the situation that the British army would face at Isandlwana in Zululand six years later, when an unprepared 24th Foot was caught in the open and destroyed to a man; the victorious Zulu impis moved on to the mission station and hospital base at Rorke's Drift. Baker's Rorke's Drift was Florence at the camp a quarter of a mile away, with the children, the sick and a small guard.

But Florence, Baker's 'little officer', was every bit as ready and determined as the defenders of the later mission. She equipped every man with a gun, even the older boys, and stationed them at the weakest points around the perimeter. She had a store of rockets angled and ready to fire at the thatched roofs of Kabba Rega's kraal.

On the parade ground, Baker ordered the troops to form square. This obsolete formation would not do on a European battlefield with cannon and explosive shells, but against spears, bows and arrows, it was still a formidable defence. The bayonets of his troops' rifles bristled outward like a hedgehog and gave the tribesmen pause for thought. Baker knew that the rifles were muzzle-loaders, and with the enemy so close, most of his men would not get off another shot.

The Bakers were inside the square, ready to give the order to fire, when Samuel saw three chiefs among the warriors milling around. He knew Rahouka, Kittakara and Matonsé, and took the gamble of his life. He and Julian walked coolly out of the square, their pistols still in their holsters. Only Monsoor, walking half a pace behind, carried a drawn sword. When a warrior's spear probed towards Baker's back, Monsoor parried it upwards with his blade. Baker now bluffed for all he was worth and started laughing. He congratulated the chiefs on their war display and suggested they have a dance. At his signal, while the tribesmen dithered, bewildered by the Englishman's sangfroid, the bugler sounded the charge and the whole square broke forward at the double. Kittakara's men fell back, overawed, and Baker ordered them all to sit down where they stood. He ordered the square to be reformed and demanded to see the king.

Unfortunately, Kabba Rega was drunk and simply reeled about at a safe distance. Kittakara backed down, offering to dance with Baker another day, when it was less hot. As Malaggé walked back to his own lines, little Cherri-Merri took his hand and walked with him.

Baker realized that he could not bluff forever. If it came to a fight, his little force would be quickly overthrown. In record time, the troops built a fort, with ramparts and ditches, but again, in a siege situation, the garrison would quickly run out of food. Baker sent out to Kabba Rega for food in the uneasy truce that followed, and he duly sent flour and cider. This peace offering was anything but. The cider was made from plantain and it was poisoned: several of the men became unconscious or had difficulty breathing. Baker and Florence, who had not drunk it, rammed large quantities of tartar emetic down the men's throats, and Florence mixed basins of mustard and salt water to make them sick. In the event, there were no deaths.

Baker sent Monsoor and a corporal to demand an explanation from Kabba Rega. It was 8 June, Samuel's 55th birthday, and shots and shouting from the long grass meant that Monsoor was under attack. The governor-general and his wife were taking a morning stroll and a sergeant walking with them was shot dead. With slow deliberation, the sort of cool that Baker's successor, Gordon, would show shortly before fanatics killed him, Malaggé buckled on his ammunition belt and took the rifle known as the Dutchman from Florence. Some of the Unyoro had rifles too, almost certainly obtained from Abou Saood, and began to fire from the tall castor-oil grass. Baker, Julian, Abd-el-Kader and sixteen of the Forty opened up on them and they soon scattered. Saat and Bellal acted as powder monkeys, dragging the ammunition boxes in the wake of the attacking Forty. As soon as they were close enough, the boys set fire to Kabba Rega's huts using blue lights, touch-papers that ignited easily, and in less than an hour the whole of Masindi was alight.

Baker withdrew as the flames roared and crackled to a height of 80 feet. It would be easy to lose sight of friends in that inferno, and the governor-general preferred to consolidate his position in the fort and count the cost so far. Four men failed to answer the roll-call, among them Monsoor, pierced with thirty-two spear wounds. 'I laid him gently on his side,' Baker wrote later, 'and pressed his hand for the last time, for I loved Monsoor as a true friend ... He was always kind to the boys and would share even a scanty meal in hard times with either friend or stranger.'[5] Ferritch Bagga had been stabbed through the chest, and the other two had died on the fort's ramparts. They were buried in new shroud-clothes, and Baker extolled the virtues of all his men.

Florence's last entry in her diary was made the day before the attack. It was 64° in the morning and 70° by midday; no work was taking place as it was Friday, the Islamic holy day. Had the battle taken another course, it would have been the last thing she ever wrote.

In the next few days, the Unyoro came back in small groups to pick over the blackened remains of their homes. At one point a spear landed in the earth feet from Baker, but he pretended not to notice. Then he made a peace offering to Kabba Rega. He sent him the musical snuffbox he knew the king coveted with the schoolteacher Ramadan and Hafiz the farrier, who both volunteered. Neither the box nor its bearers were seen again.

A further attack was beaten off on 13 June, and Baker realized he could hold on no longer. Reinforcements from Khartoum would take weeks to arrive. His only hope was fighting his way out. All night long, the women of the camp, supervised by Florence, packed as much as each person could carry at a reasonable speed. Each private carried three packs of beads in his knapsack, a sort of currency in Africa, and the heaviest load was the 64-pound box of Snider cartridges. They had two horses and three donkeys loaded with boxes, and the men poured nitrous ether, lamp oil and turpentine over the fittings of the fort and set fire to it as the column set out in a drizzly dawn on the 14th. Baker insisted the column stay intact if they were to have a hope of getting through the hostile territory, with its tall grass ideal for ambush. With the Bari guide at their head marched fifteen of the Forty with Colonel Abd-el-Kader. Behind them were ten Sniders with Baker himself, Florence, armed with elephant guns, two servants and Julian with the ammunition. Sniders were scattered along the line, with a further fifteen of the Forty bringing up the rear. The advance and rear guards as well as Baker's bodyguard carried nothing but their knapsacks and ammunition so that they were ready for action in seconds.

Florence looked back as the rearguard torched the government house. Burning in its foundations were her dresses and precious keepsakes. Perhaps Baker saw a bigger and altogether more depressing scene – his African adventure and the governor-generalship of the Nile Basin going up in smoke. On the other hand, being the kind of optimist he was, perhaps he did not look back at all. The governor-general's wife was ready for any eventuality. She carried two bottles of brandy for the wounded, two cups, two umbrellas and a locket sent to her by the Empress Eugénie, now in exile, like Florence herself, from her native country. Florence also carried a Navy Colt in her belt, and both she and Samuel knew she would not hesitate to use it.

By afternoon the inevitable attack began and the fisherman Howarti was hit by a spear, walking feet ahead of the Bakers. He clung on for days, dosed with laudanum and brandy to kill the pain, but died on the march. At least he had the satisfaction of knowing he had killed the spear's owner. By nightfall the little column had travelled only 10 miles in the tall grass: there were 70 to go. Unnecessary baggage had to be dumped – bedsteads, brandy, even Julian's uniform with its fore-and-aft hat. This was burned too – Baker intended to leave no more presents for Kabba Rega.

Two of the weak donkeys were shot and the pace picked up. On day two an ambush was launched in a marshy area, spears whizzing from nowhere until the Snider rifle fire drove back the attackers. This went on for seven days. Florence wrote later to her stepdaughters: 'I was always *so* dreadfully afraid that something would happen to dear Papa ... Everybody would have been killed without [him].'[6] Even so, she kept the last bullet in her revolver for herself. She would never become anyone's slave again. Baker's favourite horse, Zafteer, went down with a spear in its entrails which protruded from its belly. The beast stumbled on for a further 16 miles before Baker put a merciful bullet in its head.

Baker berated his troops for wasting bullets, firing at anything that moved, and called them old women. He ended up rationing their ammunition. Colonel Abd-el-Kader was wounded in the left arm. When the boy leading the last horse was mortally hit, he fell at Baker's feet – 'Shall I creep into the grass, Pasha? Where shall I go?' He died in Florence's arms.

The Unyoro imitated a bird call – 'Co-co-mé! Co-co-mé!' is how Baker wrote it down – which gave the Sniders the vital seconds to prepare for the attack, but the tension was wearing the troops down. At one point Baker was disgusted to learn that some of them had killed a tribesman, disembowelled him and eaten his steaming liver there and then to give them protection. Then they tied his carcase to a tree as a warning to any who might follow. Faddul, carrying the heaviest burden of the cartridges, reported to the pasha that he was wounded. A spear had sliced through his groin and he bled to death, given brandy to ease his passing.

After a week, the battered column reached Kisuna on the frontier of the Unyoro lands, and the attacks dwindled. They had lost ten dead and ten were wounded, and every survivor was weak with hunger and exhaustion. Somehow, Baker got the band together – a vital psychological advantage such as an instrument had not been sacrificed in the retreat – and they played all the Ottoman tunes of glory as they marched into the village. Then they dug sweet potatoes, ate and rested. 'My officers and men,' wrote Baker, 'were all delighted and overwhelmed me with compliments. I only replied by begging them always to trust in God and do their duty.'

The next day they reached Foweira and the governor-general took stock of the situation. He had three Europeans, ninety-seven soldiers, five natives, three sailors and fifty women and boys. But what of the bigger picture? Baker made overtures to Rionga, the local king, and this worked. Rionga was Kabba Rega's sworn enemy and he greeted Baker as a hero. To consolidate their new partnership – Baker would leave the king as the Egyptian government's official representative in the area – there had to be a mingling of blood; it was the African way. Reluctantly, Baker agreed, and he, Julian and the already bleeding Abd-el-Kader all went through with the ceremony.

They marched on to Fatiko, getting there on 1 August. Once again, the full dress uniforms, the bugles, the flag. Florence was riding the last horse, but Baker dispensed with his glitter, wearing the white cotton shirt, trousers and topi he had worn throughout the campaign. Abou Saood's slavers and hostile tribesmen took pot shots at them. Samuel and Julian drew up the Forty and launched a bayonet charge. Wat-el-Mek fired at Baker and missed, and 'the Dutchman had a word to say' – Baker's shot blew the slaver's gun in half and blew off one of his fingers with it. It was only with difficulty that Baker prevented Seroor of the Forty from piercing the man with his bayonet. The pursuit of the tribesmen lasted for 4 miles. The Snider rifles took their toll and the scarlet flags made easy targets, but Baker was in fact outnumbered three to one. Florence, again proving herself quite brilliant at mopping-up operations, had the prisoners rounded up under guard and all the cattle brought into the compound in case there should be another counter-attack and another siege situation developed. She even had the sangfroid to prepare a late breakfast of curried mutton and coffee for the returning Forty.

Wat-el-Mek swore undying fealty to Baker, aware that the pasha held his life in his hands, and continued his faithful service under Charles Gordon, who followed Baker. Suleiman also proved loyal. His subordinate Eddrees died of dysentery and Abou Saood disappeared, fearing Baker's vengeance.

At Fatiko the Bakers established another station – 'My country,' Baker wrote, 'was a picture of true harmony.' There were no prostitutes, beggars, organ-grinders or drunks to disturb the peace (unlike London); there were no pernickety and achingly slow law courts, and no church to stick its nose in. Baker reels off the various denominations that cluttered England, ending with 'nor even a Jesuit or a descendant of Israel to bring discord into my harmonious tabernacle'. His troops were Muslim and there was no opposing sect, although he was wrong when he claimed that 'the natives believed in nothing'.

There was plentiful shooting in his spare time, and Baker kept himself fit by regularly jumping deep ravines from rock to rock. He also wrote to Livingstone, unaware at this stage that the man had been 'found' by the journalist Henry Stanley and that Livingstone had only months to live. Emissaries came from the newly converted Muslim King M'tesa of Uganda, and by March reinforcements had come through from Ismailia. With these new men, Baker set out to fortify Fabko and Paniadoli as well as Fatiko itself. He also sent a retinue to protect Rionga.

Civilization came with these troops – 700 copies of *The Times* were brought with them and the Bakers had a chance to catch up on the news at home. All the time slaves were being freed in large batches, and a bemused Florence looked on as naked women threw themselves on their liberators. 'I found myself in the arms of a naked beauty,' Baker wrote, 'who kissed me almost to suffocation and with a moist unpleasant embrace licked both my eyes with her tongue.'

Ismailia, when they reached it on their way home, was rather run down, and the engineer Higginbottom had died some weeks previously. The Bakers said a sad farewell to their 'family' of children and the magnificent Forty, who broke ranks, crowding round their general and shouting in Arabic, 'May God give you a long life.'

In Cairo, Baker received the highest Ottoman order from the khedive and he in return gave Ismail Pasha a map showing how far south his empire now reached. From there in April he wrote to Wharncliffe: 'The slave trade is at an end – and Egypt extends to the equator.' Neither of those statements was strictly true, even though they were written by Samuel White Baker.

Chapter 12

Val's Affair

From Khartoum, Baker wrote to the Prince of Wales on 1 July 1873. The channels cut through the dreaded sudd were open and permanent (a godsend for Charles Gordon later), and the governor-general's force was in good fettle with no trace of animosity. He was rather more economical with the truth when he wrote 'the expedition that commenced with evil auspices has, thank God, closed satisfactorily in every branch'.[1]

The Bakers left Egypt in October, taking the Nubian boy Amarn with them. He would remain in the family's service in England for the rest of his life. The ex-governor and his wife were treated as conquering heroes wherever they went. They stopped off in Paris, where they were surrounded by journalists and showed Amarn the city's sights. After the siege, the Communards had burnt down the Palais de Justice, the Tuileries, the Cour des Comptes and the palace of the Légion d'Honneur; the medieval church of Sainte-Chapelle was only saved because of a faulty dynamite fuse.

If the Parisians loved Baker and the 'gentle, though heroic' woman who had again braved all hardship with him, he replaced Livingstone as the great crusader against slavery when he reached Britain. Staying in Brighton, as recommended by their doctor for their health, both of them succumbed to bronchitis in the cold fogginess of an English autumn. Reports had been coming through that they had died in Africa, not this time fighting the terrors of unchecked nature, but combating the evils of slavery. News of Livingstone's death, which reached the country at the time, only served to push Africa centre stage. *Punch*'s rival, *Judy*, carried a full-page cartoon showing a rather morose-looking Baker, with sword and map, surrounded by adoring natives. While a black-faced sphinx looks on, the ghost of William Wilberforce pats the

129

ex-governor on the back. They are both billed in the caption as 'Apostles of Liberty', and Wilberforce is saying to Baker, 'Receive a nation's thanks, with mine, for fighting freedom's cause.'

Not everyone was impressed, however, and Baker lost support when he spoke publicly at a banquet given in his honour. He spoke for Livingstone, Burton, Speke and Grant when he said that the only way to civilize Africa was to annexe it. No improvement could happen until Europeans established a firm but fair paternalistic government. Though 1873 was a little early for do-gooders to demand self-government for the natives, there was a growing group who believed that Baker had been too heavy-handed in his zeal to wipe out slavery in the Nile Basin. And no doubt his fame rankled. One correspondent who attacked him in the influential columns of *The Times* was the engineer McWilliam, who spoke of barbaric slaughters carried out by Baker. On 1 August he wrote:

> If Sir Samuel Baker wishes at any time for my testimony as to the barbarous manner in which the expedition was conducted, the wholesale murder, pillage and ruin of the country, he is welcome to it; or should the Royal Geographical Society or any body of gentlemen wish for any information regarding that futile expedition, I shall be glad to give it previous to my departure from this country.

Baker did not reply, but Julian did, on 5 August, pointing out that if a tribe such as the Bari attacked, the only recourse was to fight: 'If a military expedition is sent to annexe an extensive country, war is a natural consequence as the history of the world will testify.' Some might be left wondering what sort of expedition McWilliam thought he was undertaking, and indeed what planet he lived on. Perhaps it was just as well he was about to leave the country.

By the time Baker addressed the Geographical Society in Piccadilly in December 1873 there were effectively two armed camps: those, like the Prince of Wales, who supported him wholeheartedly, and those, fed with the distortion of McWilliam's memoirs, who saw him as some sort of avenging angel with a homicidal streak. The whole decade was one in which there was a growing sympathy for the 'noble savage' even when the disaster at Isandlwana – and in

America at the Little Big Horn[2] – might have been expected to produce the opposite emotion.

In the chair that evening was Roderick Murchison's successor, Sir Bartle Frere, one of those mavericks whom Gladstone's civil service reforms had been too late to curb. Having established a victory in the recent Zanzibar Treaty which ended slavery in that part of Africa, he would go on five years later to orchestrate what today would be seen as an illegal war against the Zulu. Baker said how glad he was that his successor was an Englishman because 'a Turk would certainly have upset the work which he had done'. This was to prove all too true in the years ahead.

The Englishman chosen to succeed Baker was the mercurial evangelist Charles 'Chinese' Gordon, and Baker must have realized that he was a better man for the job than the perfectly competent Julian, whose name he had put forward to the khedive to succeed him. In a nepotistic country such as Egypt it is perhaps surprising that Ismail did not accept the naval officer, but he knew Gordon to have that certain charisma (like Samuel) that made men follow and obey him in difficult circumstances. At first sight, there could be nothing more different than Baker and his Nile successor. Gordon was a military man, a colonel of Engineers, and was small and un-prepossessing, running everywhere at a trot with a Bible under his arm. His only vice seemed to be a fondness for brandy and soda. He accepted only one-fifth of Baker's salary and was genuinely appalled at the richness of the fittings in the Bakers' quarters in Khartoum. Above all, he was a mystic, a visionary who lived by the Bible. In other circumstances he could have been a missionary and Baker, as we know, despised such people.

Too late for the fighting in the Chinese War of 1860, Gordon nevertheless stayed in the country for four years and found himself caught up in the Taiping Rebellion, given, at the age of 30, command of the government's Ever Victorious Army and the rank of general. Little short of a military genius, he used his engineering skills to great effect, and his mysticism put the fear of God into his opponents, who dared not fire at him. A grateful government gave him the famous yellow coat and peacock's feather of a conqueror, although he declined a huge amount of cash also on offer. A quiet spell supervising forts in the Thames estuary was followed by a term improving navigation on the Danube, and it was here that he met Nubar Pasha, Ismail's foreign minister. The rest was history.

Baker and Gordon exchanged letters and met in April 1874 in a 'baton-changing' meeting. At first all was not well. Almost as soon as he reached Khartoum, where the strait-laced and quite possibly homosexual Gordon abruptly left a party where naked Sudanese girls danced in his honour, he appointed Abou Saood as his vakeel on the Upper Nile. Since Baker had left instructions that this man, the most degenerate of the slavers, should be put on trial and at the very least flogged, this seemed supreme folly on Gordon's part. It would be seven months before Gordon realized that Baker had been right and promptly fired Saood.

Baker could keep quiet no longer and wrote of his disgust to *The Times*. James Shaw, a friend of Gordon, went so far as to say that most of Gordon's problems in the Sudan came from having to undo the huge amount of harm that Baker had done. 'How it is possible,' Baker countered in a private letter to John Delaine, *The Times* editor, 'for the khedive to decorate me before parting with his highest honour – and then to speak against my acts to others without in any way having communicated his displeasure to me, is beyond my conception of Oriental morality.' Nubar Pasha, it is true, believed that Baker had been something of a bull in a china shop – 'He knew only how to drive himself hard and keep going forward' – but to an Englishman the china shop of slavery should not have existed at all.

For his part, Gordon did not share Shaw's or even Nubar's views. His time in the Sudan was as rough as Baker's, although at least, thanks to Baker, he had a navigable Nile to take him inland. Lytton Strachey sums up Gordon's difficulties well – they were exactly the same as Baker's: 'the confused and horrible country, the appalling climate, the maddening insects and loathsome diseases, the indifference of subordinates and superiors, the savagery of the slave-traders, the hatred of the inhabitants'. Baker knew all this. In a letter to Gordon in September 1875 he wrote, 'You will, I am sure, by this time have experienced that terrible strain upon the nervous system, caused by constant and annoying delays in Africa, when your spirit is craving to advance.' 'I can see how you were thwarted,' Gordon replied on 1 October:

and on my return, D.V.,[3] if I ever return, I will state my opinion publicly about your mission ... I feel so beaten down by my worries in the opening of this route that I have lost spirit ... it is *hopeless, hopeless* ever to do anything with these people.

The previous spring Baker had dashed off his *Ismailia* book. Despite the fact that it was not as popular as his earlier efforts – it dealt with the grim and sensitive issues of slavery and annexation – it still ran into five reprintings by 1890. In part, the book was written to scotch the libels of McWilliam.

From Brighton the Bakers returned to Seymour Street in London, where they felt strong enough to accept a host of invitations from friends old and new. They bought what was to be their last family home, the neo-Gothic Sandford Orleigh manor house near Newton Abbott in Devon. The magnificent views over the Teign reminded Baker of some stretches of the Nile, and while Florence organized the servants with the same flair she had in Africa, he replanted the gardens and had a palaver house built, a thatched building not unlike the government house south of Ismailia. Here were a billiard room, Samuel's guns and stuffed heads that were trophies of his various 'strolls'.

The June of 1875 saw what Dorothy Middleton describes as 'a scandal which had its day of fame and is better now forgotten'.[4] This may have been in deference to the Baker family, whose papers and reminiscences she was using, but to ignore it is to miss the point of the sexual hypocrisy of high Victorian society and to accept the fact that, were it not for the scandal, Samuel Baker might still have gone on to higher things.

For years Valentine Baker's name had been synonymous with all that was chivalrous and professional about the British cavalry. He wrote a book on tactics which was the logical successor to the pioneering work of Captain Louis Nolan[5] and another, much more political, in 1875 called *Clouds in the East*. Valentine obtained the lieutenant colonelcy of the 10th Hussars in 1860. The regiment had a flamboyant history, the uniqueness of their pouch belts giving rise to the nickname 'The Chainy Tenth', and by 1863 the Prince of Wales was their colonel. To the swagger that the regiment already had Baker brought a professionalism that lifted them into the modern era of warfare, and other regiments followed suit. No mere theorist, Baker commanded the 10th while they were stationed in Dublin at the height of the Fenian activity which led Gladstone to attempt to pacify Ireland. His flying columns of cavalry dispersed many armed and lawless risings. And it was at Aldershot in the summer of 1871 that Baker's regiment became the first to play polo in Britain – 'hockey on horseback', as *The Times* called it.

Having brought the regiment up to an unprecedented professionalism with flags for signals, pivot drill and squadron deployment, the 10th were posted to India on board the troopship *Jumna* in January 1873, and Baker relinquished command to Charles Molyneux. For a year on half pay[6] Valentine travelled to the Near East, watching the growing tensions between Russia and Turkey with some ill ease and gathering material for the *Clouds in the East*. On his return he accepted the post of assistant quartermaster-general at Aldershot, the commander-in-chief, the Duke of Cambridge, referring to him as one of the best officers in the army.

No one doubted that Valentine would go on to full general, perhaps even field marshal, and Samuel could have expected the equivalent civilian elevation at more or less the same time. All that disappeared on a Friday in the middle of June 1875 when Samuel received an urgent telegram from Valentine as he was going in to dinner with guests at Sandford Orleigh. Even before he could take a trap to the station and reach London, however, the newspapers screamed ghastly headlines – 'Extraordinary Charge of Assault'. The bottom had fallen out of Valentine Baker's life.

On the swelteringly hot afternoon of Thursday 17 June, Valentine Baker got into a first-class carriage of a train at Liphook. There were no corridor trains in 1875 – in fact what was about to happen helped to create the corridor train – and the colonel found himself in the company of 22-year-old Rebecca Kate Dickinson. Such was the extent of the scandal that was about to occur that a number of foreign newspapers took up the story. There was a piece in the *New York Times*, and most of the account below is taken from that year's *Taranaki Herald*.

Miss Dickinson had been seen off by her mother and sister at Midhurst. She was to accompany another, married, sister to Switzerland. She was sitting with her copious luggage, facing the open window to get some fresh air, when Baker got in. He began a casual conversation and they discussed a number of matters – the scenery, the London theatre scene (Miss Dickinson admired the actress Mrs Kendal) and mesmerism, a form of hypnotism already discredited by the medical world. Baker talked of the recent exhibition at the Royal Academy and sat directly opposite the woman. They had Aldershot in common; Miss Dickinson's brother was an army officer stationed there. He told her he was on the Staff.

Shortly after Woking, Baker asked her if she would be likely to ride the train again. He closed the window and asked her name, which she declined to give. He then sat beside, rather than opposite, her and held her hand. 'Get away,' she said. 'I won't have you sitting here,' and pushed him away. Undeterred, he put his arm around her waist and 'held me in front with his other arm'.[7] 'You must kiss me, darling,' he said, and kissed her. Now terrified, she struggled to ring the alarm bell but it didn't work. 'Don't ring, don't ring,' he urged. He then pinned her in the corner and kissed her on the lips, she saying 'If I tell you my name, will you get off?' 'I don't think he made any reply, but he sank down close in front of me and I felt his hand underneath my dress on my stocking above my boot.' Miss Dickinson tried to smash the window, but it wouldn't give. She stuck her head out of the window and screamed. With the train running at upwards of 40 miles an hour, no one heard. Baker was trying to pull her back, but she opened the door and clung onto the running board. He was holding her wrist begging her to get back in, and twice she begged him not to let go or she would fall.

In a bizarre conversation which could only happen in this situation in England, Kate's screams caused two men in the carriage ahead to stick their heads out of the window. 'How long is it before the train stops?' she asked. 'I don't know,' one of them said. When they reached the station, Baker told an exhausted and traumatized Miss Dickinson, 'Don't say anything; you don't know what trouble you will get me into; say you were frightened.'

Kate was shepherded into another carriage with a vicar, the Reverend Aubrey Brown, who presumably could be guaranteed not to make any advances. Henry Bailey, the guard, had noticed a commotion as the train passed the paper mills at Esher. The driver had slammed on his brakes and Bailey had blown his whistle. He remembered the lady complaining that Baker had insulted her and would not leave her alone. Bailey asked the colonel what he had done, and Baker denied any wrongdoing. Bailey locked him in a carriage with the two young men and noticed that 'his dress was then disarranged'. Baker asked to get off at Vauxhall, but was told he would have to stay on to Waterloo and would be taken to the superintendent's office.

Railway policeman Sergeant William Atter took charge of the case at Waterloo and asked Miss Dickinson what was the nature of the assault. She did not reply and the Reverend Brown said that she was in no fit state to answer questions at that time. Baker asked her if she intended to bring charges and she said, 'No'. Only now did he learn the woman's name and realized that he knew her brother quite well. He gave Atter his name and address – 'Colonel Valentine Baker, Army and Navy Club, Pall Mall and Aldershot,' and he said, a little gratuitously perhaps, 'I am sorry I did it. I don't know what possessed me to do it, I being a married man.'

A detective accompanied Valentine to check that his address was genuine and (confusingly) C. Baker, Superintendent of Police and Deputy Chief Constable of Surrey, officially arrested his namesake. By the time Valentine sent his telegram to Samuel, Miss Dickinson had undergone a change of heart. In short, someone had got to her, probably her brother, the prominent lawyer in her family; she intended to prosecute. Samuel wrote to Wharncliffe:

> As you know in such a case, a man is at the mercy of a lady, as his tongue must as a point of honour be absolutely sealed in a court of law. At the same time, Val must allow that even his best friend cannot defend even as much as he himself confesses.

And he was there at the preliminary hearing to see the court crammed with reporters and a staunch peppering of Valentine's brother officers of the 10th. One of them, Lord Valentia, put up the £1,000 surety for bail; Samuel put up the other £1,000. To Wharncliffe he confided: 'I am afraid I do feel this humiliation almost more deeply than Val himself.'

The trial was held in Croydon on 8 August 1875. That summer was quiet as far as news was concerned, and a lecherous old colonel forcing himself on a demure young lady on a train was a delicious opportunity for the scandal sheets of the day to clean up. However embarrassed the Bakers and the 10th Hussars might have been, the rest of the country loved it. The charges were twofold – indecent assault and assault with a felonious attempt (i.e. rape).

The prosecution coaxed the story out of Miss Dickinson, looking suitably chaste in a black dress with lavender gloves. On her description of Baker's hand 'underneath my dress on my stocking above my boot', her counsel asked what his other hand was doing. The (all-male) jury strained forward to catch every word. 'I had an impression,' she told the hushed, packed court. 'Nothing more.'

The Bakers had attempted to persuade Miss Dickinson to call the whole thing off; interestingly, even her soldier brother agreed with this. In the event, Baker's defence consisted merely of a statement read to the court by his counsel:

> I am placed here in a most delicate and difficult position. If any act of mine on the occasion referred to could have given any annoyance to Miss Dickinson, I beg to express to her my most unqualified regret. At the same time, I solemnly declare, upon my honour, that the case was not as it has been presented today by her under the influence of exaggerated fear and unnecessary alarm. To the evidence of the police constable [sic] Atter I give the most unqualified denial.

No one was listening. Baker was found guilty of the lesser charge. The judge, Mr Justice Brett, sentenced him to a year in prison, but without the usual accompaniment of hard labour. Miss Dickinson, according to Brett: 'goes from this court as pure, as innocent, as undefiled as ever she was – nay, more, the courage she has displayed has added a ray of glory to her youth, her innocence and her beauty.' We might be entitled to ask how safe she was likely to be in a railway carriage with the slavering Mr Justice Brett!

Valentine's family, his wife, his brothers and the entire 10th Hussars stood by him. So did the Prince of Wales, and that gives a clue as to what really happened in that hot summer of 1875. What was really on trial in Croydon was, on the one hand, the whole sweaty strait-jacket of Victorian morality and on the other the country's increasing antipathy to the heir to the throne. Valentine Baker was a member of the 'Marlborough House Set', the coterie of the prince and the Duke of Sutherland. Such men were obscenely rich, spoiled and expected to take whatever they wanted, as if by right. Sir Frederick Johnstone was a connoisseur of women and wine; the Marquess of Waterford eloped with the wife of his best friend; Lord Hartington was renowned for his string of mistresses, as was Bertie; the Marquess of Hastings lost a fortune at cards by his early death in his mid-twenties. Those who supported Baker went so far as to suggest that it was Bertie on that train and that the colonel was nobly covering for him, forgetting the 8-inch disparity in their height.

Baker was cashiered from the army and on his release from prison was informed that the queen no longer had need of his services. But the widow at Windsor had gone further than that. Her lack of rapport with Bertie's profligate lifestyle was well known, but she gave him nothing important to do. She had never approved of Samuel Baker, sharing Lady Login's view that he was not the right chaperon for the impressionable Duleep Singh all those years before. Neither had she approved of the way in which Samuel had acquired Florence. She meted out the same disdain to Lord Cardigan, the hero of Balaclava, when she had herself brushed out of an oil painting showing him explaining the Charge of the Light Brigade to her and Albert; there is only a dark patch in the existing version today. And when Samuel suggested in the nicest possible way that he and Florence might be presented at court, he was told it was unlikely and he should not ask again.

In an unprecedented move, the queen wrote personally to Miss Dickinson, expressing regret at her ordeal and asking for a photograph of her. In her narrow and bitter mind, it was not Valentine Baker who was in the carriage, but her son, Bertie, who had caused the death of his father, Victoria's beloved Albert. 'No court today,' wrote Michael Brander in 1969, 'would have accepted such unsupported evidence' as that given by Kate Dickinson. 'With modern psychiatric knowledge every court, policeman and probation officer is familiar with the common wish-fulfilment fancies of young females, the hysterical self-delusions which often lead to a genuine belief that they have been attacked and nearly raped.'[8]

A vigorous counsel today would demolish Miss Dickinson's testimony, having dug into her background, obtained psychiatric reports and so on. That was not how it was done in 1875. An officer and gentleman did not call a lady a liar. And the use of language is so twee that it is impossible now to decide exactly what did happen in that railway carriage. As to Baker's charge that the railway policeman was lying about his comments to him, that is entirely likely. The Metropolitan Police were notoriously corrupt: the entire detective branch was dismissed two years later in an orgy of fraud and bribe-taking.

The one piece of evidence that sunk Baker was the reference to his dress being disarranged. This presumably means his fly-buttons, and it was his contention that they popped open while he was struggling to save Kate Dickinson's life, that she had, in her panic, torn them open as she grabbed at him. 'I always knew that the "trousers" would be the fatal point,' Samuel wrote to Wharncliffe.

In March 1876, as Valentine came to the end of his time in prison and various journals like *The Sporting Times* had very much taken his side, Samuel wrote to Wharncliffe to thank him for visiting his brother in gaol, and commented drily: 'I believe the title [of Valentine's *Clouds in the East*, the publication of which had been delayed] includes "Explorations of unknown parts in Central Asia". I hope the result will be more happy than his exploration of "unknown parts" in a railway compartment.'

Others were able to stand back and put the whole thing in perspective. Captain Ronald Wingate, who served under Valentine, wrote: 'On 2 August 1875 a foolish old judge and twelve good tradesmen and true had condemned Lieutenant Colonel and Brevet Colonel Valentine Baker of a crime which was not a crime and his country had no further use of his services.' Even his enemy in 1877, the Russian general Shavolov, wrote: 'Poor Baker was the finest Light Cavalry Officer I ever saw. Had he belonged to me do you think we would have lost him to the service he adorned because of a wretched private folly?'[9]

But the actual upshot of Valentine's career crash was best commented on by a Turkish officer who saw him in action in 1878 against a vastly superior force of Russian cavalry: 'And yet Allah has smitten the English with such mad blindness that they allow a man like him to leave their army.' And no one was madder over the affair of the colonel than Samuel White Baker.

Chapter 13

The Traveller

In many ways Samuel and Florence Baker made the perfect lord and lady of the manor. He became president of the Devonshire Association and stood on the Newton Abbot town council. The family often visited, and Samuel told tall tales of Africa to his nieces, one of whom wrote: 'Our visit could not have been jollier. It has also taught us many things. I hope we shall try and follow Aunt Florence's methodical ways.'[1] And Florence's firmness remained. When a little boy stayed at Sandford Orleigh and took against the butler, kicking him in the ankle, he was sent to bed by the mistress of the house on a bread-and-water diet. 'Servants are our friends,' she told him. 'We don't kick our friends.' Samuel could be even more severe. When 'Eddie', the Prince of Wales's eldest son, and his brother George came to stay, Baker caned them both for breaking branches of a rare tree they had been told not to climb; George would go on to become King George V.

After all her adventures, the life of a lady suited Florence. She would go 'up to town' with or without Samuel for great occasions, and they usually rented a town house for the season to make this easier. But for the explorer, the governor-general, the man of action, Devonshire was rather tame. He continued to hunt vigorously and maintained his superb arsenal of hunting guns. On one occasion, when a strong man came to Newton Abbot and invited members of the audience to have a go at breaking his chains, Baker did – and snapped them with his phenomenal strength.

Above all, Africa called to him and he read the papers avidly for any news of Gordon, as well as maintaining a regular correspondence with him. The new governor-general kept to the Nile (which he could, now that the sudd was under control) and took command of Baker's Forty again, having to fight off the Bari just as before. On

1 September 1878 Gordon wrote to Baker: 'How I wish you were here in my place with all my worries and bored to death! ... Now we have two steamers on the Lake [N'yanza] ... Come up and write another book ... Telegraph to me that you will come; start at once.'

It was very tempting, especially as it had been Baker's dream to see steamers on Lake Albert and they were *his* vessels. But he had made a promise to Florence. He replied to Gordon on 16 October: 'I should not hesitate for an instant, personally; but she [Florence] is, I know, afraid that, if once I get into the old groove, my visit would be prolonged; and she rather dreads a return to savagery.'

In the meantime, events were moving on elsewhere. In 1875 the khedive had been forced to declare himself and his country bankrupt, and to recoup at least some of his losses he put up for sale his share of the newly opened Suez Canal. Disraeli, now prime minister, saw this as a golden opportunity to seize a global initiative in terms of trade. Britain's merchant navy was the biggest in the world and control of the canal would give her huge prestige and profits. He could not persuade his Cabinet, however, so took the extraordinary step of approaching his old friend the millionaire banker Lionel de Rothschild, who provided a massive personal loan. In one sense the gamble was a triumph in that British world trade expanded enormously, and the canal sounded the death-knell of the sail-driven clipper ships that brought wool and dairy goods from Australasia; the canal had no wind and no tide. On the negative side, however, whoever controlled the canal had to control Egypt, and the knock-on effect of this was a generally painful experience for Britain right up to the humiliation of the Suez crisis of 1956.

In 1877 the build-up of tension between Russia and Turkey that Valentine Baker had prophesied in *Clouds in the East* erupted into a declaration of war. The tsar, Alexander III, was every bit as pushy and aggressive as his forebears, and it looked as though the Crimean War was about to be played out again. The Russians had already, as early as 1871, rebuilt the naval base of Sebastopol, prompting many Englishmen to wonder what the Crimea had been for.

Since Valentine and Samuel both had important friends in Turkey and the ex-colonel was surplus to requirements, Valentine was given the rank of major-general in the Turkish army – there was a Baker Pasha on the world stage again. He may not have been Baker of the Tenth any more, but he was still 'the man on the white horse', a charger given to him by the Prince of Wales.

A war correspondent at the Battle of Taskhessan at the end of 1877 wrote that he could not help:

> watching the man on the grey Arab and I saw his sabre go sweeping up and down and all round like lightning flashes. He made a lane through the ranks of the Russian infantry in whatever direction he went ... There was no holding back Baker and his Turks and the Russian cavalry was soon tearing back as hard as they could go, to get under the shelter of their guns ... I saw a shell explode within a few yards of the Pasha; his horse fell and down he came. That was the end of the grey Arab, but not his master, for Baker was up in a moment on the charger of a common trooper, in the middle of his men, hacking like a very Hercules. The old Artillery officer who was standing close by me, laid down his field glasses and said 'I swear by the Prophet that the Infidel who commands our cavalry fights with the courage of a thousand tigers.'[2]

Perhaps Valentine felt he had something to prove. The rearguard action against the Russians lasted for ten hours and gave the man no longer on the white horse worldwide renown. He returned on leave and was given a banquet at Stafford House in London by the Duke of Sutherland. Samuel was there, but it was a men-only occasion in case wives and sweethearts still felt any lingering sympathy for Kate Dickinson. At the suggestion of the Prince of Wales the next morning, the Marlborough Club decided unanimously to reinstate Valentine, who, with his wife, Fanny, spent a few days with Samuel and Florence at Sandford Orleigh.

Back in Turkey by May 1878, Valentine, who may well have been a better writer than Samuel, was reorganizing the outdated Ottoman army and starting work on his next book, *War in Bulgaria*. A few months later Samuel and Florence were on their travels again. He was 57 now but as strong and vigorous as ever, and they began a sort of grand tour which was the next best thing to 'strolling' in dangerous places. They would travel in comfort, not wading waist-deep in stagnant water and fighting off natives, but their wanderings reveal a fascinating snapshot of world events at the end of the 1870s.

The first stop was the Mediterranean island of Cyprus. From here, Baker wrote to Gordon:

> I should have liked to run up and see you at Khartoum ... It was very kind of you, my dear General Gordon, to invite Lady Baker (with myself and Julian) to come and see you; and she hopes some day to see you in our own home in England, instead of in Central Africa.

Disraeli's masterly handling of the ongoing Eastern Question throughout 1878 had led to the Congress of Berlin in which European statesmen brought a halt to the Russo-Turkish War, checked Russian aggression and prevented a Europe-wide war on the scale of the Crimean. One of the perks that Britain received was Cyprus in exchange for an annuity of £92,000 and it proved crucial. The Mediterranean could fairly now be claimed as 'our sea'[3] since Britain possessed Gibraltar, Malta, Cyprus and access to the Red Sea via the Suez Canal.

The island itself was an unknown quantity to most Englishmen. It was generally held to be unhealthy, and Baker bought a caravan to tour the place, with a wagon to carry their luggage and supplies. Amarn went with them, as did three spaniels to accompany Samuel on the hunt. All of it was detailed in *Cyprus as I Saw It in 1879*, which Baker subsequently wrote; he enjoyed the careful ordering of the caravan as much as he had that of the government house in Ismailia. Colonel Warren, the first governor, was already westernizing the place. Roads and bridges were either built or under construction, and marshes had been drained. By the time they arrived, Kyrenia, the nominal capital of the island, had a post office, telegraph and hospital.

At Larnaca, which they reached on 4 January 1879, they found the newly built Craddock's Hotel, which exceeded all expectations. The mountain roads soon took their toll on the caravan, however, and the undercarriage had to be considerably strengthened. They hired mules for riding and took on drivers and a Greek cook, Christo, and the multilingual Georgi. Game was scarce, because every Cypriot, whether Greek or Turk, carried a gun and hunted regularly. Even so, Baker was able to bag partridge and hares. He was aware of tensions between the ethnic groups on Cyprus which would spill over into civil war years later. Everyone was kind, however, and the Bakers stayed at Government House in Lefkosia (today's Nicosia), which would become the island's capital years later. Here lived one of Victoria's most capable generals, Garnet Wolseley and his wife. Wolseley's career had crossed with both Valentine Baker's and Gordon's.

Wolseley had served in the Crimean War and had fought in Burma, the Indian Mutiny and China. Having to live down the fact that he was a shopkeeper's son (something of an obstacle even after the abolition of the purchase system for officers in 1871) he spent ten years in Canada before a successful campaign in the Ashanti War in Africa. By the mid-1870s he proved himself an exceptionally talented officer and drew around him 'the Ring', an elite group of staff officers. He was the blueprint for W.S. Gilbert's 'very model of a modern major-general' and had a reputation of being a fixer. A few weeks after playing host to the Bakers, he was sent out to sort out the mess that Lord Chelmsford had got himself into against the Zulu. His knack for putting things right led to the phrase 'all Sir Garnet' creeping into the language by 1880.

The Bakers loved Kyrenia, but thought little of its wine, transported as it was in goatskin sacks over rough terrain. Limassol, with its flourishing salt and carob exports, was clearly destined to become Cyprus's industrial centre, and was the next port of call where the Bakers made rather unlikely guests perhaps at the Greek Orthodox monastery of Trooditissa. True to form, although the monks were filthy in their personal dress and their buildings, Baker set about growing neat gardens and getting the monks to wash during their three months there.

In today's world, war-torn Beirut might seem a strange destination, but in 1879 the Bakers found simply a small Turkish town on the way, as it turned out, to the ancient and fascinating Damascus. Their original plan had been to visit India, but news of a famine in the interior caused a delay. Damascus was not that safe either. Nineteen years earlier an estimated 3,000 Christians had been massacred there by Muslim fanatics. They saw Jerusalem, whose very cosmopolitan nature gave it its instability. It was the holiest city in Palestine, revered as such by Christian, Muslim and Jew, and had of course been the target of crusaders for centuries. There were Russians there in large numbers, as well as Egyptians, Frenchmen and Italians.

The Bakers, their dogs, their luggage and Amarn then crossed the Mediterranean to Port Said. This vital coaling station for the merchant ships of empire was only twenty years old when they arrived. It was of course linked with the Suez Canal, Said Pasha being the enterprise's most vociferous supporter. The town and port stood on land reclaimed from the sea by French engineers.

Then began the sea voyage to Madras. There seems to be no firm suggestion that the Bakers should put in at Colombo. The family still retained the estates there at Newera Ellia, but perhaps Baker wanted to have new experiences rather than revisit the old. Madras, on Edward Lear's coast of Coromandel, was one of the three presidencies of the East India Company. By the 1850s it had become chief port of the Deccan and the viceroy, when in residence as he was from time to time, lived in the Government House. The new observatory regulated time and issued weather reports all over India and Ceylon.

By the time the Bakers reached India, the reverberations of the mutiny were dying away. Conversely, true Indian nationalism was only around the corner: the first Congress met in 1885. Disraeli had won a symbolic victory in 1877 by suggesting that Victoria be given the title Empress of India. In every city in the subcontinent the Bakers would have seen statues and portraits of the woman whose pettiness had helped to damage the family's reputation. On the surface, the Raj seemed secure, not least in the railway network that now criss-crossed India. The natives had got used to the *ag-gari*, the fire-carriage, and this was how the Bakers arrived at Poona, in the old Bombay presidency on the west coast.

Poona was the residency of the viceroy in the hot season and had an important military base at Kirkee, where a steeplechasing course had been built by Colonel William Morris of the 17th Lancers back in 1858. The city bristled with Maratha temples and bustled with its flourishing manufactures – gold, silver, cotton, paper and flour.

By February 1880 the Bakers had reached Baroda, still in Bombay, and were entertained by the Gaiknar (ruler) with falconry displays and shooting. The native princes of India had been allowed to retain the trappings of wealth without having any authority. Sumptuous entertaining and hospitality was a cornerstone of their lifestyle. What particularly interested Baker was the use of cheetahs for the hunt. They were carried on specially constructed carts and had their heads covered as with a falcon's hood until their black buck prey was in sight. Baker had never seen cheetahs in action and certainly not working for man:

> Suddenly there shot up a heavy cloud in the midst of which we discerned the wrestling figures ... When we galloped to the spot, we found the noble buck upon its back and the cheetah, fixing its relentless grip upon the throat of its prize. The race was over [after a mere 400 yards].

The next stop was Allahabad in the north, on the left bank of the river Jumna where it met India's holiest river, the Ganges. The Bakers were now in the heart of mutiny country. The first attack on the whites had occurred at nearby Meerut on 10 May 1857 and spread throughout Bengal. Only in Delhi, which the Bakers visited next, was there any appreciable civilian involvement, perhaps because there were no British troops there at the time. Delhi was not yet India's capital; that was Calcutta, site of the infamous 'Black Hole' from the days of another native uprising, that of Suraj-ad-Dowlah in 1756.

By the time the Bakers were touring Bengal, the heat was stifling, but with their African experience (and in the case of Samuel, Sinhalese) this meant nothing. Samuel shot a magnificent tiger and was 'met with a splendid charge. My new .577 double rifle is a beautiful weapon and closed his account on the spot.' This was written in a letter to Wharncliffe, and it is clear that the Bakers were riding elephants at the time.

From India the party made its way to Hong Kong, which had been ceded to Britain in 1841 and was a crown colony. The island itself was only 11 miles long and 5 miles wide, but a narrow strip of the Chinese mainland at Kowloon had been annexed in 1860. The Chinese were a secretive, isolated people, suffering only limited contact with the outside world. Of the country's ports, only Canton was open to trade with the West. Its very isolation was a challenge to the Western powers, and their presence an irritation to the government. Quite willing to employ foreigners such as Charles Gordon when it suited them, the forces of conservatism in the country later focussed on the Boxers, the 'fists of righteous harmony' who clashed with the 'foreign devils' in Peking in 1900.

The Bakers took in the sights of Canton and Shanghai before sailing for Japan. Here they spent eight months and were fascinated by this strange land with its blend of ancient and modern. They were probably not aware of how fast the country was westernizing. The older generation of samurai, the knightly class, still wore armour and their women walked humbly several paces behind them. On the other hand, the docks at Nagasaki were being rebuilt to accommodate modern merchantmen and the steam-driven iron-clad warships that would spectacularly destroy the Russian fleet in the 1904–05 war. And in the same city, the year before the Bakers arrived, the Meiji government had set up the country's first college for women. The place had only been open to foreign trade for twenty years at this point.

While Florence bought beautiful porcelain and bronzes, Samuel acquired a number of weapons and a full suit of armour, all to be shipped home to Sandford Orleigh. He also did a lot of hunting, especially of sambur deer and pheasant. He wrote to Wharncliffe of the large Russian presence in the area, aware that Russian ports were frozen for months of the year, whereas those of Japan were not. To men of Baker's generation, Russia was infinitely more dangerous than any other country, as events of the last three years had proved. It must be watched.

From Yokohama, the Bakers set sail for a world as different from all they had seen as chalk from cheese. They reached San Francisco, a city that had been little more than a vast, sprawling mining camp for some years. It formally became American in 1846, and the discovery of gold three years later meant that California became a Mecca for all the get-rich-quick merchants from all over the world. It had a large and thriving cosmopolitan population, with Japanese and Chinese ghettoes and a Latin quarter. The area known as the Barbary Coast was a huge red-light district where gangs of drunken sailors roamed the streets. A kind of stability had been imposed by 1856 when vigilantes set up kangaroo courts and hanged offenders.

Most of the wooden houses, shops and hotels that the Bakers knew would be destroyed by the earthquake of 1906.

The Bakers made for the hinterland in search of game. For a few years now, European aristocracy had passed this way adding to the wholesale slaughter of the buffalo which once roamed the plains in vast numbers. Civilization in the form of the railroad threatened the way of life of these herds as well as that of the native Americans who relied on them for food and clothing. The Bakers went into the Rockies, travelling as far as Rock Creek by the Union Pacific Railway.

They were unconsciously stepping into a way of life that was coming to an end. The forty years after the American Civil War formed the nucleus of the Wild West, a time and a place turned into legend by Hollywood. Learning to ride a Western saddle, which must have felt something like an armchair, Baker cantered through the waving grasses of the Big Horn mountains. Only five years earlier, General George Custer and his 7th Cavalry had been wiped out in these rolling hills. The victors of that lop-sided engagement were now being rounded up on reservations, to the eternal shame and embarrassment of the American people.

On the way to Fort Fetterman, one of the cavalry outposts that protected the white settlers who had poured into the Black Hills after the gold strike of 1874, the Bakers found the trading posts filthy and the beds full of bugs. The fort itself was worse. Major and Mrs Powell were hospitality itself, but the place had a jangly, nervous feel about it. Only days earlier, the commanding officer, Colonel Gentry, had acted as coroner in the inquest of a man shot down during a game of cards. Such things did not happen in the British empire.

'Castle' Frewen, 20 miles away, was a log cabin, the heart of the Frewen ranch, which boasted 8,000 head of cattle. Another day, by jolting buggy, got the Bakers to another ranch, that of Mr and Mrs Peters. Extraordinarily, there was a telephone line from here to the Frewen ranch. Some 4,000 feet up on the Rosebud river, the Bakers met their hunting guides. Jem Browne and Texas Bill were the leaders, men who knew the trails and the ways of the diminishing buffalo herds. Gaylord was the wrangler in charge of the horses, and the cook was a German called Henry.

It was to the disgust of Browne that Baker refused to kill more than a token number of animals. 'I cannot shoot to waste,' he wrote later, 'therefore upon many occasions I declined to take the shots.' There was no situation here in which he could leave the carcase to grateful natives, as he had in Africa. They were living on oatmeal and maize on the reservations. 'Several parties of Englishmen,' Baker noted, 'had not been as merciful.' Browne scoffed, 'If you came all the way from the Old Country to shoot and you won't shoot when you've got the chance, you'd have done better to stop at home.' Baker sacked him.

He did find some sport, however, with Big Bill, a Swede, and Little Bob, a Scotsman, who were camped nearby. Bob in particular was the fastest skinner of animals Baker had ever seen. They hunted bears and deer. Samuel was very impressed by the Colt .45 pistols he saw in use. These legendary guns were known as Peacemakers and Thumb-breakers, and when he got home, Baker ordered a pair from his London gunsmith.

By September it was snowing in the Rockies, and time for the Bakers to leave. The world had turned again and Africa still called to Samuel White Baker.

Chapter 14

The Journey Taken Alone

Events in Egypt caught the attention of the outside world in 1881, while the Bakers were still in the Rockies. The khedive was officially bankrupt by 1879 and his country fell under the dual control of Britain and France. Since Britain already effectively ran the Suez Canal, French interest in the area waned, and within two years Egypt was British. As Sir Charles Dilke said in the Commons in July 1882:

> As regards the Suez Canal, England has a double interest; it has a predominant commercial interest, because 82% of the trade passing through ... is British and it has a predominant political interest caused by the fact that the Canal is the principal highway to India, Ceylon, the Straits and British Burma ... and also to China, where we have vast interests, [and] to our Colonial empire in Australia and New Zealand.[1]

The rise of Arabi Pasha threatened all that. Ismail had been replaced in 1879 by his son Tewfik, and Colonel Arabi was war minister in his Cabinet. He was a nationalist – his slogan 'Egypt for the Egyptians' has been hijacked countless times since his day – and he particularly detested the French. Attempts to dismiss the man led to riots in Alexandria in June 1882, and more than fifty Europeans were killed. Part of the tragedy for Egypt and the Sudan in these years was the vacillating nature of Gladstone's second ministry. William Gladstone was a giant intellect who strongly disapproved of imperialism, which he labelled contemptuously Beaconsfieldism (Disraeli's earldom was Beaconsfield), and Disraeli was dead.

Because of the distances involved and the relative slowness of communication, however, much depended on the men on the spot. In the summer of 1882 that was Admiral Seymour, whose ironclads smashed Arabi's newly built defences at Alexandria. A joint Anglo-French force was to be sent to put the colonel's revolt down, but a change of government in France caused the French withdrawal, and Garnet Wolseley, ever the fixer, did it alone. Landing in August with 35,000 men, he crossed the desert by night marches and routed Arabi's army at Tel-el-Kebir. Here were 4 miles of entrenchments and 26,000 rebels, but after only an hour's fighting Arabi's men ran.

Tewfik was restored, but it was clear that the khedive was simply a British puppet. The real power in Egypt was the high commissioner, Sir Evelyn Baring, and he watched with unease the nationalist movement growing to the south. Mohammed Ahmed ibn el Sayyid Abdullah called himself the Mahdi, the messiah, and raised the flag of *jihad* over the desert. Arab fundamentalism has become more familiar in recent years, but the British of the late nineteenth century had no experience of it. The Mahdi, inevitably labelled 'mad' by every Englishman, intended to drive the Europeans out of the Sudan, and his rapidly growing supporters were imbued with the fanaticism of the holy warrior.

Samuel Baker knew very well the truth of the old Arab saying – 'When Allah made the Sudan, he laughed' – and so did Charles Gordon. Both men watched as the Mahdists not only grew in numbers but scored success after success. Egyptian police sent to arrest the Mahdi were murdered, and in January 1883 he stormed El Obeid, the capital of the desert area called Kordofan. This gave him a large arsenal – five cannon and 6,000 rifles – and the British sent Colonel William Hicks to stop him in his tracks. Hicks was an intelligent man, but he did not know the desert or the Mahdi. Effectively lost in the wilderness of Kordofan with his uncertain troops weak with thirst and exhaustion, he was caught out by the rebels and his command wiped out. The Mahdi's prize in the Hicks disaster was four Krupp guns, ten mountain guns, six Nordenfeld machine guns and 8,300 rifles, but psychologically more important was the head of a British colonel, and it drew thousands more supporters. In the east, the Mahdi's right-hand man, Uthman Diqna (Osman Digna) besieged the Egyptian outpost at Suakin.

The destruction of Hicks would have led earlier sabre-rattlers such as Palmerston and Disraeli to bring down the wrath of God on the head of the Mahdi, but Gladstone, the liberal, could see no cause for intervention, and merely decided to send a single individual to evacuate Khartoum and the other garrisons which would be the Mahdi's ultimate objectives. The question was: who should go?

Gordon had been succeeded as governor of the Sudan by Raouf Bey, who had shown his incompetence and had given a lacklustre performance under Samuel Baker when he held the post. Worse, his number two was the ex-slaver Abou Saood, and between them, paralysed by the Mahdist uprising, these two proved the correctness of Baker's pronouncement to the khedive nine years earlier that the governor-general should be an Englishman. By the time the post was given in the middle of 1882 to Abd-el-Kader, the competent colonel of Baker's Forty, it was already too late.

At the same time Valentine had been offered the post of commander-in-chief of the Egyptian army. If Victoria could not get over the railway carriage incident, others were eager to use his services. He took his wife and girls out to Cairo and set about reorganizing and training the men accordingly. When he asked for British officers to be sent out to command the battalions, however, the old problem arose. Officers could not serve under anyone who had been cashiered, and the queen still stubbornly refused to reinstate Valentine. Letters flew in all directions, but the upshot was that Valentine should command the gendarmerie, a combination police-cum-militia. It was ironic that he had resigned his generalship in the Turkish army to become a glorified policeman and that he had brought his family out to Egypt – his wife and elder daughter would die out there, as would he, some said, of a broken heart.

In the winter of 1882–83, Samuel and Florence went to Egypt, staying on the *diahbiah Osprey* on the Nile. Samuel's daughters Agnes and Ethel were with them and they spent time with Valentine and his family. It was while they were there, however, that news reached them of the death of Samuel's favourite brother, John. He had gone back to England for an operation but it was not successful, and he had died soon after his return to Newera Ellia, now a thriving tea plantation, Mahagastotte.

Between them, Samuel and Valentine knew exactly how to contain the Mahdi problem, but Valentine was not actually in command, and this led to the Hicks debacle. On 30 November 1883, Lord Dufferin, the high commissioner before Baring's appointment, wrote to Samuel, now back in England, admitting that his (Baker's) strategy was superior. On 4 January of the following year, Charles Gordon, by this time in Brussels, also wrote to Samuel proposing that he and Valentine go out to the Sudan, one as civil, the other as military governor. Gordon was serious, and he came to Sandford Orleigh to press the point.

The same month Baker met his successor at Newton Abbot station and took him on a two-hour drive around the Devon countryside. Gordon had by this time received news of Gladstone's decision – he was to be the man to evacuate the Sudan garrisons. But it was not a job he wanted. He had been asked by King Leopold of the Belgians to undertake an administrative post in the Congo. 'I do not want,' Leopold wrote to one of his ambassadors, 'to miss a good chance of getting us a slice of this magnificent African cake.'[2] 'Gordon was magnetic and compelling,' Robin Baily, Baker's nephew, wrote later, and by the time the ex-governor had arrived at Sandford Orleigh for tea, Baker was all for it. What would have happened if the project had gone ahead? With the evangelical Gordon in the Congo, the appalling exploitation of the natives would surely have been kept to a minimum. The bigger question is would Baker have lost Khartoum and died a martyr as Gordon was to do? I believe that he would have largely followed Gordon's path; Samuel Baker was no martyr, but he would not simply roll over when the Mahdi told him to. He would have died on the palace steps at Khartoum, but would have taken more fanatics with him than Gordon did.[3]

In the event, Florence stepped in. When the men brought up the subject over tea, she said, 'Sam, you promised me you would never go back to the Sudan without me. I do not go. So you do not go.'

The bachelor Gordon was flabbergasted that a mere woman could call the shots at Sandford Orleigh. To order a household was one thing; to dictate the destiny of empire was something else. Baker meekly said to the man later in the day, 'My dear Gordon, you see how I am placed – how can I leave all this?' No one has ever seen this as a sign of cowardice, least of all Gordon, and at that point the Mahdi's noose had not yet tightened around Khartoum to make the whole venture pointless. Baker was a man of duty and principle, but no one in officialdom had approached him, and he had seen the government in its various manifestations kick Valentine in the teeth so often, he may not have seen the Sudan, ultimately, as any of his business.

On 16 January he wrote to *The Times* expressing his delight at Gordon's appointment. He was the right man for the job. Gordon himself contacted Baker, grateful for any hints (he spoke no Arabic, for example), and expected to be back in four months.

In the meantime, the Egyptian regime had imposed on Valentine to take the field to relieve Suakin, with his motley gendarmerie. This had been Samuel's fear. The previous November he had written to his brother: 'Let nothing persuade you to attempt the passage of the Suakin Desert with such troops, otherwise you will share the fate of Hicks.' The letter had not arrived before Valentine marched out on 15 December, but he hardly needed Samuel's warning. His troops had to be cajoled into leaving Egypt, and Valentine knew perfectly well that they would collapse against the Mahdists, despite his training of them and personal leadership. Recruits for this army had literally been grabbed from the streets of Cairo and marched in chains to the barracks – hardly the best way to begin a campaign. Sir Evelyn Baring promised to provide food and supplies and Zobieir Pasha also pledged his support. But Zobieir was an ex-slaver and Gessi, Gordon's number two when he had been governor, had had the man's son executed. In the event he gave no help at all.

General Baker Pasha had 1,000 of his gendarmerie, 450 Turkish and Egyptian cavalry and 1,500 black troops. Against him, Osman Digna had 20,000 fanatics, all of them experienced soldiers. On 8 January, he wrote to Fanny in Cairo: 'They have sent down nothing, no boats, no telegraph, no Turks, no anything!' Then Fred Burnaby of the Blues walked into his camp. He had obtained leave from the Royal Horse Guards, and at Baker's request turned up to ride with him. This tall, gallant officer was the epitome of the dash and sangfroid of the sons of empire. A painting by James Tissot shows him sprawled in his mess dress, enjoying a cigar. The Sudan would claim his life too.

The Battle of Tokar could be nothing but a disaster, given the quality of Valentine's troops and the lack of support from Cairo. The panicky Egyptians at one point opened fire on Baker and his staff as they tried to rally them. Fred Burnaby wrote later: 'General V. Baker and Colonel Hay with the Arabs between them and the Egyptians, forced a passage through their foes – Egyptians on their knees praying for mercy; English and foreign [Turkish] officers at the guns, surrounded by their assailants, selling their lives dearly.'[4] Valentine was the last man to leave the field, and even then had to be dragged away by Fitzroy Hay. Again, the losses of matériel were huge. Two Krupp guns, two Gatlings, two rocket troughs and 2,000 rifles were now in the hands of Osman Digna, and Suakin remained as tightly besieged as ever.

Fanny Wormald, Fanny Baker's cousin, was in Cairo and covered the events of those tumultuous days in her diary. 'Sir Samuel and Lady Baker arrived here on Saturday,' she wrote, 'too late, alas, to be able to help.'[5]

Help eventually came from the obvious quarter. News of the 'Suakin business' reached Britain and, despite Gladstone's continued opposition, an army was sent out under General Stephenson, reaching the area by 22 February. Valentine was appointed chief intelligence officer. Samuel kept his brother as cheerful as possible during those days, staying with Florence on the *diahbiah Hermione*. On the 26th he received a telegram from Gordon – 'Hope all is well. Sorry Suakin business. Tell your brother, heads or tails up here! but will trust.' Three days later, the beleaguered ex-governor was still trying to persuade Baker to join him – 'We are all right up here for present. You and Lady Baker would enjoy the excitement. It is a question of weeks (?) but hope to pull through.'

Whether Samuel and Florence argued over this we do not know. He was clearly in Egypt to lend moral support to Valentine, but was he also intending to travel south to Khartoum? Stephenson's army moved against Osman Digna at the village of El Teb. Valentine Baker commanded the infantry square and was delighted that the 10th Hussars, who had been re-routed to the area on their way home from India, were fighting alongside him. Two weeks after the battle, *Punch* captured the poignancy of the moment in a poem, 'A Tale of the Tenth Hussars':

> On the Staff as the troopers passed it, in glorious pride and
>   pluck,
> They heard, and they never forgot it, one following shout 'Good
>   luck!'

Wounded and worn he sat there, in silence of pride and pain,
The man who had led them often, but was never to lead them
again.
Think of the secret anguish – think of the dull remorse,
To see the Hussars sweep past him, unled by the old white
horse.

As so often the British troops were outnumbered at El Teb and their losses were heavy – Major Slade and Lieutenant Probyn were among the officers of the 10th killed that day. Valentine was hit in the face and calmly had the wound dressed before returning to the action. That night a naval surgeon on board the *Sphinx* took forty-five minutes to remove a 2-ounce iron ball from his cheek. Fred Burnaby had his horse shot from under him and was hit in the arm by shrapnel.

Among the many heroes at El Teb one who stood out was Trooper Hayes, an ex-boxer who rode with the 10th Hussars. He saved a wounded comrade on foot and, having lost his sword, proceeded to knock seven bells out of the Mahdists with his fists. When presented with personal thanks by General Stephenson, Hayes asked if there was any chance of Baker being restored to them. As *Punch* put it:

Then the general smiled, 'Of course,
Give back to the Tenth their Colonel, the man on the old white
horse.'

But it was never to be. Back in England in May, Valentine needed specialist treatment for the face wound and was hailed as a hero at Charing Cross station.

Samuel and Florence had gone back the previous month, Baker having received the ribbon of the Medjidie order from the khedive. He lost no time in starting an appeal via *The Times* to put as much pressure on Gladstone as possible to save Gordon. Everything moved with impossible slowness as Gladstone began to realize that Gordon intended to make a stand at Khartoum rather than evacuate it, which had been his initial orders, and such was the pressure of Baker and his lobbyists that he eventually sent Garnet Wolseley to do his usual job of fixer. Even so it was not until November that Wolseley's force reached Dongola on the Nile. Baker had been consulted on the best sort of transports to use and Julian, now a commander, was with Wolseley's naval accompaniment.

On 12 December, Wolseley wrote to Baker: 'Events on the Upper Niles [the Mahdi's continued advance] are marching quickly and what the end is, or how we are to get out of the false position the folly of Gladstone has forced us into, is more than anyone can say.' Six weeks later, Gordon was dead and the Mahdi's Koranic flags fluttered over the ramparts of Khartoum. Sir Charles Wilson's relief column got there two days too late. 'I shall never publish another remark concerning Egypt,' Baker wrote, perhaps feeling more than a fair share of guilt, 'Now that poor Gordon is sacrificed I ... remain a passive spectator of the misery and shame that have been the result of British interference.' At home, Gladstone's popularity plummeted and the G.O.M (Grand Old Man) became the M.O.G. (Murderer of Gordon).

Sorrows began to crowd in on the Bakers. As part of the relief expedition to Khartoum, the British army fought the Mahdists at Abu Klea in January 1885. Fred Burnaby died there, a spear through his throat. The moment was captured by one of the most haunting verses of the century, from Henry Newbolt's 'Vitae Lampada':

The sand of the desert is sodden red –
Red with the wreck of a square that broke –
The Gatling's jammed and the Colonel dead,
And the regiment blind with dust and smoke,
The river of death has brimmed his banks
And England's far and Honour a name,
But the voice of a schoolboy rallies the ranks:
'Play up! Play up! And play the game!'

It is unlikely that Valentine and Fanny Baker felt like playing the game any more. A week before Abu Klea, their eldest daughter, Hermione, never strong, died. She was 18 and her funeral, beside the Nile in Cairo, was attended by the gendarmerie, the 19th Hussars and over 100 carriages. The gold locket she had given to Captain Kitchener was worn by the man on his own last journey on HMS *Hampshire*, when the ship was sunk by a German mine in 1916. A month after the funeral, her heart no doubt broken, Fanny Baker died too.

With all this, Samuel and Florence could not face a return to Egypt that year, so they sailed for India for some tiger shooting with the Rajah of Suchi Khan on the Brahmaputra. Back in England by the spring of 1886, despite his vow to write nothing more on Africa, Baker began an active campaign to win the Sudan back from the Mahdists. The Mahdi himself had died of natural causes only months after Gordon, but his successor and his followers, increasingly known as 'Fuzzy-Wuzzies' by the British troops because of their wild hair, effectively ruled all the Sudan, and might even threaten Egypt itself.

The Bakers spent the winter of 1886/87 in Egypt with Valentine, whose remaining daughter, Sylvie, now 17, was with Samuel's daughters Ethel and Agnes, on their way to Ceylon and Mahagastotte. In November 1887, by which time Samuel and Florence were back home, Valentine became depressed and ill. He watched the sunset from the deck of his *diahbiah* on the 16th and went to bed. Early the next morning, he was complaining of pains in his chest, and, despite doses of laudanum, died quietly in the middle of the morning.

There was an outpouring of grief in Cairo and all over Egypt, and magnificent tributes appeared: 'The favourite of society, the dashing cavalry officer, the lion of so many a gay coterie, has died far away from friends and home and it is in a foreign land that his old comrades pay the last honours to his name.'[6] Even the bitter old queen had relented, bowing at last to pressure from all quarters to reinstate Valentine into the British army. Unfortunately, he never knew that. Rather like Gordon, the relief that might have saved his life did not arrive until it was too late.

The last years of Samuel Baker's life remained as busy as ever. He packed on weight now and realized that his days of hunting were nearly over. Lords Dufferin and Cromer (Evelyn Baring) often consulted him on Sudanese matters. Stanley kept up a regular correspondence on all matters African, as did Richard Burton; both men had shared something of Baker's extraordinary experiences. Roland Ward, proprietor of a taxidermist business in Piccadilly with an international reputation, constantly asked the great man's views on how animals should be displayed and mounted, sending the odd specimen for the palaver house.

And the Bakers still travelled. They were in India in 1888, coursing with dogs Cabre and Mora, and the following year in Jabalpur, where Baker began his last book, *Wild Beasts and Their Ways*, a lively mix of hunting tales, including the American experience, and animal behaviourism.

But slowly things were shutting down and the end of an era was approaching. Baker's third daughter, Constance, had died in 1883 and Agnes, perhaps the most like her father in temperament, died in childbirth at Mahagastotte. Edith and Ethel were at Sandford Orleigh when the news broke, and Florence was perfect in comforting them all. By 1890 Baker was nearing 70 and suffering from gout. The chilly, damp Devon winters did not suit him, and the couple were in India and Egypt up to 1892. One of the last letters he wrote was in reply to the Countess of Stradbroke, declining an invitation to visit her country house at Henham:

> I cannot tell you how my heart sinks when I acknowledge that 'the spirit is willing but the flesh is weak'. Those who were born in 1821 cannot be like those born at a later and more reasonable date. I have no fear of hot countries, but the cold keeps me indoors. It is quite possible that I may be off next year – perhaps to shoot lions in Somaliland or on some such errand.[7]

But the errand that Samuel Baker went on on 30 December 1893 was one that he had to undertake alone. The pains in his chest were identical to those experienced by Valentine. It was a heart attack. Julian, visiting at the time, went to London to fetch a specialist, but he was too late. Baker murmured to Florence, 'Flooey, how can I leave you?' These were the last words of Samuel White Baker.

Chapter 15

The Boy's Own Hero

The year in which Samuel Baker died was a world away from that in which he had been born. In the continent he knew so well, the Union flag flew in Uganda, and a force under Dr Leander Jameson crushed a revolt by the Matabele tribe. The Transvaal annexed Swaziland, and a French protectorate was established in Dahomey. When the Germans put down a native revolt in East Africa, it was clear that the scramble for Africa, once a steady stroll, was now a headlong gallop.

In the science and technology Baker had so loved as a boy, American surgeon David Williams performed the first open-heart surgery, on a knife victim. The man lived for twenty more years. The French inventor Léon Appert invented glass reinforced with wire mesh, and a American industrialist, Henry Ford, was testing a gasoline-powered internal combustion engine which would revolutionize the world. Karl Benz was doing much the same thing in Germany. Astonished Londoners gawped up at Alfred Gilbert's statue *Eros*, a monument to the factory reformer Lord Shaftesbury, and the first in the world to be made of aluminium. Norwegian artist Edvard Munch exhibited *The Scream*, a painting that has haunted its viewers ever since. The Coca-Cola Company was registered in America, and William Wrigley introduced Juicy Fruit and Spearmint to his range of chewing gum; by 1910 it would be the top-selling brand in the United States. Among those who died in the same year as Baker were Pierre Beauregard, the Confederate general; Guy de Maupassant, the French writer; John Rae, the Arctic explorer; and Peter Tchaikovsky, the Russian composer. Those who were born in 1893 entered a world Baker would not have understood and would probably not have much liked. Two of the future leaders of Nazi Germany, Hermann Goering and

161

Joachim von Ribbentrop made their first appearance; so did the future war poet Wilfred Owen and America's sweetheart, the actress Mary Pickford.

In the ever-revolving stage of world history in which the many players have their entrances and exits, what was the role of Samuel Baker? In a letter to his sister Ellen in September 1862 he wrote: 'You know what I always was – made up of queer materials and averse to beaten paths; unfortunately not fitted for those harnessed positions which produce wealth; yet, ever unhappy when unemployed and too proud to serve.' Men such as Baker do not fit easily into society. They defy categorization. Baker was a Victorian, yet he was born before that era began. He was an explorer, an administrator, a soldier, a statesman, a husband, father, brother and son. He farmed, he rode, he organized, he hunted, fought and killed – both animals and men – and he did all these things without regret because they were a series of challenges he could not resist.

One problem with a man as Renaissance as Baker is that he is all things to all men. The various biographies of him try to paint a balanced picture of the explorer and administrator. Some, notably Michael Brander's, see him first and foremost as a hunter and naturalist. And in the sense of pure exploration, he has to take his place, perhaps, behind Speke, Burton, Grant and in particular Livingstone – the best-remembered discoverers of Africa. Had Baker been allowed to go, as he asked, with Livingstone to the Zambezi in 1858, he might well have been at the head of the queue. He had to concede that Speke had found the larger lake – the Victoria N'yanza – and that his own success, the smaller Albert, was not the great inland sea he thought it was.

In the sense of administration, he has to stand a little behind Gordon too. The hard spadework was carried out by Baker, but it was Gordon who actually ended the slave trade, and his martyr's death at Khartoum gave him, conversely, an immortality that Baker, dying quietly in his bed, could never manage. But what if the original plan had worked out and the vengeful queen had not been involved? What if Samuel and Valentine *had* controlled the Sudan between them? Could they have stopped the Mahdi? We will never know.

The other problem with evaluating Baker is the astonishing speed of change since his death. Shooting wild animals today is condemned, and is illegal throughout Africa except in rigidly controlled conditions. Elephant poachers, who kill the great beasts for their ivory, are criminals today – they were businessmen when Samuel Baker knew them. No one has stuffed lion or leopard heads on their lounge walls, and very few antique shops still sell such trophies.

But it is not the business of historians to apologize for the past. Neither should we use today's yardsticks by which to measure anyone. We must view Samuel Baker in the context of his own time and among his own people, starting with the obituaries that followed his death, leading on to the entry in the *Dictionary of National Biography* and his first full biography, *Sir Samuel Baker: A Memoir*, written by Douglas Murray and Silva White in 1895. As is often the case with obituaries, they are generic and eulogistic and often pose more questions than they answer. *The London Illustrated News*,[1] for example, states quite matter-of-factly that Baker married Florence in 1860. It also describes his education as 'desultory'.

In 1890 Baker received a letter from Dr Edvard Schnitzer, the enigmatic German who, as Emin Pasha, ran the southern Sudan from 1878 to 1884. He wrote:

> You were not forgotten amongst my men, who never wearied of telling their young comrades the story of Sir Samuel (as they call you) and his daring feats. In Bunyoro, also, you are remembered ... The natives ... have very often spoken to me of 'The Morning Star' as they call [your wife] up to this day ... At M'tesa I saw a picture of lady Baker and yourself.

This was the sort of praise that pleased Samuel, coming from men who actually knew the score. He was remembered in the Sudan until the 1960s, when archaeological digs were taking place there.

At his request, Samuel Baker was cremated, ironically at Woking, with its associations with Valentine's fated train journey. The debate over cremation versus interment had been raging for twenty years, but all the Bakers except Florence were horrified by it. His ashes were placed in the crypt beside his father's tomb at Grimley, near Worcester. Sandford Orleigh, all its fittings and his belongings, plus the ongoing royalties from his writing, went to Florence during her lifetime, even with a separate annuity so that should she remarry she would never be dependent financially on another man.

Not that there was much chance of that. Flooey was heartbroken by the death of her husband. To her he had been her rock for more than thirty years, and they had hardly ever, in that time, been apart. However else we judge Samuel Baker, his was one of the great love stories of the nineteenth century. Florence lived on as 'Grande Dame and Hausfrau' of Sandford Orleigh, doted on by Samuel's extensive brood of grandchildren. One of them, Robin Baily, went on to join the Sudan Political Service, and when on leave he would tell Florence, in the Arabic tongue they both spoke, of the grandsons of the men the Bakers had known along the Nile.

Florence died quietly, reunited with her Sam, on 11 March 1916. The guns were thundering at Verdun and the death of a lonely old widow hardly merited a mention. *The Times* wrote: 'Baker – On the 11th March, at Sandford Orleigh, Newton Abbott, Florence Mary Barbara, wife of the late Sir Samuel Baker, aged 74.' On her death, the great estate was sold and broken up, and the Bakers' possessions were scattered to members of the family and beyond. Until recently, items of uniform and horse furniture belonging to Valentine were on display in the National Army Museum, Chelsea. Samuel's letters today fetch in the region of $200. The obituaries and the biographies focus, inevitably, on Africa and on Baker's achievements in that unlucky continent. He was essentially a man of his time, and men are not made like that any more. Today's hunters stalk their game with cameras, not rifles, and now television allows us all to be world travellers and experts on big game. Today's administrators are university men (and women) in suits, bound by the restrictions of political correctness and in touch with their governments by modern means of communication. The British have no empire left and there are millions who have no wish and in many cases no capability to understand exactly what that empire was.

The best epitaph that anyone could write for Baker came from an anonymous Sudanese who spoke for his generation and perhaps for all time:

He came to rule us; we knew nothing, he taught us. When we wanted to play, he played with us. When we had to fight, he fought with us and showed us newer ways. When we wanted to hunt, he hunted with us. When we were sick, he nursed us. And when we sinned, he shook us until our teeth dropped out.[2]

No one could describe better the man who was Samuel White Baker.

Notes

Chapter 1. The White Man's Burden

1. Baker, *Eight Years' Wandering*.
2. Sri Lanka today.
3. Baker, *Eight Years' Wandering*, p. 271.
4. From Rudyard Kipling, 'A Tale of Two Cities'.
5. The London street containing the East India Company's head-quarters.
6. *The Works of John Ruskin*, vol. 20, London, 1905, p. 42.
7. Parliamentary Papers, vol. 7, 1837.
8. Charles Darwin, *The Voyage of the Beagle*, London, 1839 (diary entry, 12 January 1836).
9. Richard Cobden, letter to Edward Ellice, 1856. Quoted in *Speeches on Questions of Public Policy by Richard Cobden MP*, ed. John Bright, Macmillan, 1878, p. 248.
10. Alfred Milner, *The Milner Papers*, vol. 2, *South Africa*, 1933, p. 467.
11. Arthur de Gobineau, *Essay on the Inequality of the Human Races*, 1855. Quoted in M.J. Cohen and John Major, *History in Quotations*, London, Cassell, 2004, p. 681.
12. *Edinburgh Review*, vol. 41, 1850, p. 61.
13. *Anthropological Review*, vol. 4, 1866, p. 120.
14. I call him this because his Criminal Law Amendment Act of 1884 made homosexuality an offence punishable with prison. He took no action on child prostitution or prostitution in general.
15. Henry Labouchere, 'The Pioneers' Hymn', quoted in Cohen and Major, *History in Quotations*.
16. George Bernard Shaw, *The Man of Destiny*, 1895, in *Plays Pleasant and Unpleasant*, vol. 2, London, 1898, p. 20.

17. In the decade after Samuel Baker's death this bestowal was called the *Pax Britannica*, the British Peace. Nowadays, with American help, it is called regime change.
18. *The Expansion of England*, lecture 1, 1883, quoted in Cohen and Major, *History in Quotations*.
19. Baker, *Albert N'yanza*, vol. 1, p. 288.
20. Baker, *Eight Years' Wandering*, p. 273.
21. Baker, *Eight Years' Wandering*, p. 274.
22. Baker, *Eight Years' Wandering*, p. 277.
23. Winston Churchill's famous description of Gandhi.

Chapter 2. The Bakers' Half-Dozen

1. Brander, *Perfect Victorian Hero*, p. 12.
2. From Samuel Baker's diary, quoted in Middleton, *Baker of the Nile*, p. 22.
3. Middleton, *Baker of the Nile*, p. 22.
4. Middleton, *Baker of the Nile*, p. 23.
5. Quoted in Brander, *Perfect Victorian Hero*, p. 13.
6. The period saw experiments in electrical attempts to resuscitate the dead. Mary Shelley's Gothic horror story *Frankenstein* (1818) was merely an imaginative take on something believed to be possible.
7. Quoted in Brander, *Perfect Victorian Hero*, p. 14.
8. Quoted in Brander, *Perfect Victorian Hero*, p. 15.
9. Murray and White, *Sir Samuel Baker*, quoted in Middleton, *Baker of the Nile*.
10. Brander, *Perfect Victorian Hero*, p. 17.

Chapter 3. Newera Ellia

1. The Victorian age was notorious for its large families. Without effective contraception, pregnancy was very likely, especially in well-to-do families with good food, fresh air and a modicum of medical care. Henrietta's contemporary Queen Victoria famously dreaded pregnancy and detested babies. Doing her duty for her country (although she found sex with Albert no problem) led to a total of eighty-one months of pregnancy.
2. Mark Twain, *Following the Equator: A Journey Round the World*, 1897, ch. 62.

3. Baker, *Eight Years' Wandering*, p. 16.
4. Baker, *Eight Years' Wandering*, p. 18.
5. Baker, *Eight Years' Wandering*, p. 19.
6. Baker, *Eight Years' Wandering*, p. 23.
7. Quoted in A. Baker, *Question of Honour*, p. 6.
8. Baker, *Eight Years' Wandering*, p. 30.
9. Baker, *Eight Years' Wandering*, p. 32.
10. Baker, *Eight Years' Wandering*, p. 37.

Chapter 4. Eight Years' Wandering

1. Baker, *Eight Years' Wandering*, p. 40.
2. Baker, *Eight Years' Wandering*, p. 65.
3. Baker, *Eight Years' Wandering*, p. 70.
4. Baker, *Wild Beasts*, p. 29.
5. Khaki means 'dust-coloured' in Persian, and after years of unofficial use was adopted by the British army for service dress in 1898.
6. Baker, *Eight Years' Wandering*, p. 106.
7. Shotguns, unlike most other firearms in the UK, may be legally held.
8. Baker, *Eight Years' Wandering*, p. 108.
9. Brander, *Perfect Victorian Hero*, p. 37. Throughout the century, hunters and the armed forces carried all but the kitchen sink with them. Regimental silver accompanied the army on campaign, but the Coldstream Guards had to leave theirs behind on the dockside on embarkation to the Crimea when they realized the troopship could not accommodate it.
10. Baker, *Eight Years' Wandering*, p. 130.
11. Brander, *Perfect Victorian Hero*, p. 46.

Chapter 5. Taking a Stroll

1. Middleton, *Baker of the Nile*.
2. Quoted in Edith Sitwell, *Victoria of England*, Boston, Houghton Mifflin, 1936, p. 212.
3. Edward Bauernfeld, *Memories of Old Vienna*, 1923, p. 274, quoted in Cohen and Major, *History in Quotations*, p. 558.
4. Sandor Petöfi, *Life or Death*, September 1849, quoted in Cohen and Major, *History in Quotations*, p. 559.

5. Franz Grillparzer, 1849, quoted in Cohen and Major, *History in Quotations*, p. 559.
6. G.M. Trevelyan, *British History in the 19th Century*, London, Longmans, Green, 1924, ch. 19.
7. Messalina was the murderous wife of the Roman emperor Claudius. Her name is a byword for avarice, lust and cruelty.
8. The surname was that of a friend of his, the son of Lord Leven.
9. Middleton, *Baker of the Nile*.

Chapter 6. 'Flooey'

1. Nicolas de Nicolay, *Dans l'empire de Soliman le Magnifique*, ed. M.-C. Gomez-Géraud and S. Yérasinos, Paris, Presses du CNRS, 1989, p. 83.
2. Hall, *Lovers on the Nile*, 1981, p. 39.
3. Quoted in Middleton, *Baker of the Nile*.
4. Middleton, *Baker of the Nile*.
5. *The History of Romanian Railways*, http://www.cfr.ro/cfr_new/eng/istorie.htm.
6. Brander, *Perfect Victorian Hero*, pp. 56–7.
7. Quoted in Hall, *Lovers on the Nile*, p. 55.
8. Quoted in Hall, *Lovers on the Nile*, p. 60.
9. Quoted in Hall, *Lovers on the Nile*, p. 65.
10. Shipman, *Stolen Woman*, p. 26.

Chapter 7. Into the Dark Continent

1. Quoted in Hall, *Lovers on the Nile*, p. 73.
2. Quoted in Hall, *Lovers on the Nile*, p. 13.
3. The holiest shrine of Islam in the Great Mosque of Mecca. It is the centrepiece of the *haj*.
4. Baker, *Albert N'yanza*.
5. It was not that far removed in fact from the white slave auction in which Samuel had met Florence. The bizarre difference is that the woman actually paid the man in the form of her dowry and wedding expenses.
6. The firman was an official letter which could be presented to other rulers in the African world, ensuring Baker every assistance. It could of course be ignored.

7. Baker, *Albert N'yanza*.
8. Baker, *Albert N'yanza*.
9. Baker, *Albert N'yanza*.

Chapter 8. The Lake of Dead Locusts

1. Collins, *The Nile*, p. 1.
2. Although not necessarily. There was no age of consent as yet in Britain, as the journalist William Stead proved when he caused a deliberate scandal by 'buying' a girl of 13 in 1885.
3. Not only did the plumes appear attached to the headstalls of undertakers' horses, but undertakers' mutes carried whole trays of them on their heads.
4. In 1898 at Fashoda, when French and British forces claimed the same village, there was a real risk of war.
5. Quoted in Hall, *Lovers on the Nile*, p. 128.
6. It would be fascinating to know if this was the stars and stripes or the new Confederate stars and bars.
7. Middleton, *Baker of the Nile*.

Chapter 9. 'Sacrifices to Geography'

1. Baker, *Albert N'yanza*.
2. Baker, *Albert N'yanza*.
3. Middleton, *Baker of the Nile*.

Chapter 10. Baker Pasha

1. Baker, *Albert N'yanza*.
2. Quoted in Hall, *Lovers on the Nile*, p. 356.
3. S.W. Baker, *Ismailia*, London, Macmillan, 2 vols, 1874.
4. Snook, 'Myth of Native-Bashing'.

Chapter 11. Dancing with Baker

1. Quoted in Hall, *Lovers on the Nile*, p. 362.
2. Baker, *Ismailia*.
3. Baker, *Ismailia*.
4. A sort of foreman.
5. Baker, *Ismailia*.
6. Quoted in Hall, *Lovers on the Nile*, p. 388.

Chapter 12. Val's Affair

1. Quoted in Brander, *Perfect Victorian Hero*, p. 142.
2. See Chapter 13.
3. Deo Volens – God willing.
4. Middleton, *Baker of the Nile*, p. 254.
5. Nolan's book on cavalry appeared in 1852, and senior officers (Nolan was a mere captain) were outraged at the man's arrogance.
6. The government's cynical way of saving money. Officers' pay was never enough for the expense of the social round anyway.
7. Trial transcript as quoted in the *Taranaki Herald*.
8. Brander, *The 10th Royal Hussars*, p. 56.
9. Quoted on cover of Baker, *Question of Honour*.

Chapter 13. The Traveller

1. Quoted in Hall, *Lovers on the Nile*, p. 424.
2. Baker, *Question of Honour*.
3. The Romans had an exactly equivalent phrase – *nostrum mare*.

Chapter 14. The Journey Taken Alone

1. Parliamentary Debates, July 1882, vol. 272.
2. Leopold II to Henri Solvyns, 1876. Quoted in Cohen and Major, *History in Quotations*, p. 691.
3. The moment of Gordon's martyrdom is shrouded in mystery. The perceived wisdom as shown in the painting by George William Joy and re-enacted in the Charlton Heston film is that the unarmed Gordon, with his cane and Bible in hand, put up no personal resistance and was speared to death. Mahdist sources suggest that he emptied his pistol at his attackers.
4. Quoted in Baker, *Question of Honour*, p. 140.
5. Quoted in Baker, *Question of Honour*, p. 141.
6. *The Times*, quoted in Baker, *Question of Honour*, p. 171.
7. Quoted in Brander, *Perfect Victorian Hero*, p. 169.

Chapter 15. The Boy's Own Hero

1. 6 January 1894, p. 5.
2. Quoted by Mrs Hyde Baker, in Middleton, *Baker of the Nile*, p. 270.

Select Bibliography

Baker, Anne, *A Question of Honour*, London, Leo Cooper, 1996.

Baker, Samuel White, *The Albert N'yanza*, London, Macmillan, 1866.

——, *Cast up by the Sea*, London, Macmillan, 1869.

——, *Eight Years' Wandering in Ceylon*, Philadelphia, Lippincott, 1875.

——, *Wild Beasts and Their Ways*, London, Macmillan, 1890.

Beckett, I.F.W., *Victoria's Wars*, History in Camera Series, London, Shire, 1974.

Brander, Michael, *The 10th Royal Hussars*, Famous Regiments Series, London, Leo Cooper, 1969.

——, *The Perfect Victorian Hero*, Edinburgh, Mainstream, 1982.

British Empire, 1497–1997, London, *Daily Telegraph*, 1997.

Collins, Robert O., *The Nile*, Connecticut, Yale University Press, 2002.

Cowles, Virginia, *Edward VII and His Circle*, London, Hamish Hamilton, 1956.

Hall, Richard, *Lovers on the Nile*, London, William Collins, 1981.

James, Lawrence, *Rise & Fall of the British Empire*, New York, St Martin's, 1999.

Judd, Denis, *Empire*, London, HarperCollins, 1996.

Keegan, John, and Wheatcroft, Andrew, *Who's Who in Military History*, London, BCA, 1976.

Kipling, Rudyard, *Definitive Edition of Rudyard Kipling's Verse*, London, Hodder & Stoughton, 1977.

Knight, Ian, *Go to Your God Like a Soldier*, London, Greenhill, 1996.

Middleton, Dorothy, *Baker of the Nile*, London, Falcon, 1949.

Morris, James, *Pax Britannica: The Climax of Empire*, London, Folio Society, 1992.

Murray, Douglas, and White, Silva, *Sir Samuel Baker: A Memoir*, London, Macmillan, 1895.

Shipman, Pat, *The Stolen Woman*, London, Transworld, 2004.

Snook, Lt. Col. Mike, 'The Myth of Native-Bashing', *BBC History Magazine*, vol. 9, no. 1, January 2008.

Strachey, Lytton, *Eminent Victorians*, London, Chatto & Windus, 1921.

Times History of the World, London, *Times*, 1999.

Williams, Neville, ed., *The Changing World*, vol. III, *1776–1900*, Oxford, Helicon, 1999.

Index

Abbai, 97
Abd-el-Kader, Col., 111–28, 153
Abdullah (cook), 118
Abdullah, Major, 117
Abou Do Roussal, Sheikh, 77, 78
Abou Saood, 114, 117, 120, 121, 123,
　126, 127, 132, 153
Abou Sinn, Achmet, 76
Abu Klea, battle of, 158
Aden, 70, 87
Affudo, 117
African tribes
　Bari, 83, 115, 117, 118, 119, 124, 130,
　　141
　Basé, 78
　Basuto, 66
　Bedouin, 76
　Bishareen, 76
　Bunyoro, 93
　Buranda, 88
　Dinka, 86
　Galla, 77
　Hadendowa, 76
　Hamran, 77
　Har Owel, 68
　Laboré, 118
　Latooka, 91
　Loquia, 115
　Matebele, 161
　Obbo, 91
　Shilluk, 113
　Shookerijah, 76
　Shuli, 115, 119
　Zulu, 4, 8, 65, 122, 131, 145
Agad & Co., 114, 119
Aggageers, 77

Ahmet Agad, 114
Albert, Lake – see Luta N'zige
Albert Nyanza: Great Basin of the Nile,
　103, 104
Albert, Prince Consort, 50, 79, 101,
　108, 138
Aldershot, 134, 136
Alexander III, Tsar of Russia, 142
Alexandria, 72, 99, 106, 151–2
Ali Nedjar, 118
Aliwal, battle of, 50
Alma, battle of, 48
Amarn, 118, 146
Arabi Pasha, 151, 152
Army and Navy Club, 136
Arnold, Thomas, 17
Aswan, 72
Athenaeum Club, 103
Atholl, Duchess of, 54
Atholl, Duke of, 46
Atter, Sgt. William, 136
Austro-Hungarian Empire, 4, 15, 27,
　51

Bacheet, 75, 78
Bagnères-de-Bigorre, 46
Bailey, Henry, 135–6
Baily, Robin, 58, 154, 164
Baines, Thomas, 103
Baker, Agnes, 102, 153, 158, 160
Baker, Ann, 15, 16, 102
Baker, Beatrice, 58
Baker, Charles, 21–2, 24
Baker, Constance, 102, 160
Baker, Edith, 47, 52, 102, 105, 160

Baker, Elizabeth (nee Martin), 21, 26, 46

Baker, Ellen, 15, 162

Baker, Ethel, 102, 153, 159, 160

Baker, Fanny, 143, 155, 156, 158

Baker, Florence, 55–64, 65–98, 101–3, 104, 105, 106, 107–28, 129, 133, 138, 141–50, 153, 154, 156, 157, 159, 160, 163, 164

Baker, Henrietta (nee Martin), 21, 24, 25, 26, 45, 46, 47, 49, 59

Baker, Hermione, 158

Baker, James, 15, 47, 48, 49, 63, 101

Baker, Jane, 26

Baker, John (16th century), 11, 16

Baker, John, 3, 15, 18, 19, 21, 27, 28, 35, 40–1, 47, 49, 95, 153

Baker, Louisa, 101

Baker, Lt. Julian, 110–28, 130, 144, 160

Baker, Mary (Min), 15, 60, 61, 65, 102, 105

Baker, Mary (Samuel's mother), 45

Baker, Richard, 12

Baker, Samuel (Sir Samuel's father), 13, 14, 27, 45

Baker, Samuel, 1, 2, 3, 4, 5, 6, 7, 8, 9, 10, 12, 45, 47, 48, 49, 52, 53, 54, 55, 58, 59, 60, 61, 62, 63, 64, 105, 106, 129, 130, 131, 133, 136, 138, 139, 161–5

  childhood, 14–19

  death, 160

  governorship of the Sudan, 107–28

  hunting, 33–43

  in Ceylon, 21–43

  knighthood, 104

  last years, 151–60

  Nile expedition, 65–98

  wedding, 101–3

  world tour, 141–50

Baker, Supt. C., 136

Baker, Sylvie, 159

Baker, Thomas, 15, 17

Baker, Valentine (18th century), 12, 13

Baker, Valentine, 3, 15, 18, 28, 31, 35, 47, 48, 49, 56, 63, 66, 79, 105, 133–40, 142–4, 145, 153–7, 160, 162, 163, 164

Balaclava, battle of, 48, 138

Banks, Joseph, 66

Baring, Evelyn, Lord Cromer, 152, 154, 155, 159

Barklay, George, 61

Barklay, Henry, 61, 62, 63

Barklay, Jack, 61, 62

Barklay, Robert, 61

Barnes, Edward, 26

Barrake, 77, 78

Bashi-Bazouks, 48, 69

Bauernfeld, Edward, 51

Beaufort, Duke of, 41

Behrens (banker), 19, 24

Bellal, 118, 123

Bem, General, 59

Bengal, 2, 147

Berbera, 68, 73, 74

Berlin, 53

'Big Bill', 150

Bingham, James, Lord Lucan, 33

Bloomfield, Col., 37

Bombay, 2, 146

Bonaparte, Napoleon, 23, 46

Bosphorus, 49

Bowie, Col. James, 34

Breadalbane, Earl of, 50

Breslau, 53

Brett, Mr Justice, 137

Bristol, 13, 21

British Anti-Slavery Society, 86, 93, 108, 109

Bronnell, Clarence, 82

Brown, Rev. Aubrey, 135, 136

Browne, Jem, 149

Brudenell, James, Lord Cardigan, 33, 138

Brunel, Isambard Kingdom, 21

Bucharest, 58, 59, 60, 61, 72

Budapest, 51, 53

Buganda, 94
Burma, 3, 4
Burnaby, Col. Frederick, 155, 158
Burton, Col. Joseph, 67
Burton, Richard, 56, 65, 67–70, 88, 98,
    100, 130, 159, 162
Burundi, 81
Buxton, Thomas Fowell, 5, 7

Caesar (Black Joke), 12
Cairo, 72, 103, 106, 107, 110, 128, 153,
    155, 156, 158
Cambridge, Duke of, 134
Cambridge University, 18, 101, 109
Canada, 4, 15
Cape of Good Hope, 6, 21
Caroline of Brunswick, 14, 67
Cassala, 74, 75
Cast up by the Sea, 62, 105
Castle Menzies, 50
Cetewayo, 8
Ceylon, 1, 3, 6, 8, 9, 15, 21–43, 45, 46,
    49, 66, 72, 73, 74, 87, 146, 159
Charge of the Light Brigade, 48
Chartism, 27, 28
Chelmsford, Lord, 145
Cherri-Merri, 121, 123
Chilianwallah, battle of, 50
Christo (cook), 144
Clapham, J.H., 99
Clarendon, Lord, 66
Clark, Adam, 53
Clifton, 21
Clumsy, 85
Colombo, 9, 24, 25, 26, 29, 30, 34, 52,
    146
Colquhoun, Robert, 61, 72, 73, 97, 99
Compagnie des Indes, 2
Congo, 154
Congress of Berlin, 144
Congress of Vienna, 23
Constantinople, 58, 63–4
Constanza, 60, 61, 62, 63, 67, 71

Corn Laws, 34
Cornwallis, Charles, 12
Crimea, 47–9, 51, 57, 66, 69, 82, 106,
    116, 142, 144, 145
Croydon, 136, 137
Cuckoo, 118, 119
Custer, Gen. George, 149
Cyprus, 144–5
Cyprus as I Saw It in 1879, 144

Dalhousie, Lord, 50
Damascus, 145
Danube, 52, 54, 58, 61
Danube and Black Sea Company, 60,
    63, 70
Darwin, Charles, 5
de Bono, Andrea, 87
de Gobineau, Arthur, 6
de Montenac, Lt., 26, 35
de Rothschild, Lionel, 142
Delaine, John, 132
Derby, Earl of, 104
Dickinson, Rebecca, 134–9, 143
Dilke, Charles, 151
Disraeli, Benjamin, 3, 18, 28, 104, 110,
    142, 144, 146, 151, 152
Djaffer Pasha, 111, 112
Dobson, Mary – *see* Baker, Mary (Sir
    Samuel's mother)
Dobson, Thomas, 14
Dongola, 157
Dufferin, Lord, 153, 159
Duleep Singh, Maharajah, 49–59, 138
Dunster, H.P., 18–9

Earl of Hardwick, 29
East India Company, 2, 3, 49, 67, 146
Eddrees, 120, 127
Edward (Bertie), Prince of Wales, 50,
    52, 54, 56, 106, 129, 130, 133, 137,
    138, 141, 143
Edward VI, 11, 16

Egypt, 4, 68, 71
Eight Years' Wandering in Ceylon, 38, 45
El Obeid, 152
El Teb, battle of, 157
Emin Pasha (Dr Edvard Schnitzer), 163
Enfield, 14, 16
Engels, Friedrich, 15
Esterhazy, Duke, 53
Ethiopia, 81, 84
Eugénie, Empress of France, 100, 125

Fabko, 115, 120, 127
Faddul, 126
Fad-el-Kereem, 118
Fairfund, 21, 24, 26
Faloro, 115
Fashoda, 112
Fatiko, 115, 117, 118, 119, 121, 126, 127
Ferritch Bagga, 124
Fitzhardinge, Lord, 41
Fladbury, 45
Foweira, 115, 120, 126
Fowler (bailiff), 28
Fowler, Mrs, 31
Frankfurt, 19, 52
Franz Josef, Emperor, 53, 58, 86
French Empire, 15
Frere, Bartle, 8, 131
Funchal, 13

Galentz, 53
Galton, Francis, 95
Gaylord (wrangler), 149
Gedge, Dr, 114
Gentry, Col., 149
George IV, 14–5, 67
Georgi (driver), 144
Gessi, Deputy Governor of Sudan, 155
Gibbs, George, 34
Gilbert, W.S., 145
Gladstone, William, 8, 104, 131, 134, 151, 152, 154, 156, 157, 158

Gloucester School, 18
Gondokoro (Ismailia), 82, 84, 86, 88, 97, 112, 115, 116, 117, 127, 128, 144
Gordon, Charles, 108, 117, 123, 127, 129, 131–3, 141–2, 144, 147, 154–8, 162
Grant, Capt. James, 70, 82, 87–9, 99, 100, 101, 103, 104, 130, 162
Green, Charles, 20
Grillparzer, Franz, 51
Gurkhas, 2

Hafiz (farrier), 124
Haggard, Rider, 65
Haleem Effendi, 73
Hanim, Finjanjian, 59
Harar, 68
Hartington, Lord, 138
Hastings, Marquess of, 138
Hay, Col. Fitzroy, 155–6
Hayes, Private, 157
Henry (cook), 149
Hicks, Col. William, 152, 153, 155
Higginbottom, Edwin, 111, 114, 119, 128
Highnam Court, 17, 21
Hill, Rowland, 20
Hodgson, Thomas, 5
Howarti (fisherman), 125
Huxley, Charles, 70, 100

Ibrahim, 91
Ibramiyeh, 117
Indian Mutiny, 3, 28, 51, 88, 145, 147
Isandlwana, 122, 130
Ismail Pasha, Khedive of Egypt, 106, 107–9, 131, 132, 151, 157
Ismailia, 112, 120, 133

Jack, 21
Jali, 74
Jameson, Dr Leander, 161

Jarvah, 118
Jerusalem, 145–6
Johnstone, Frederick, 138
Jumna, 134

Kabba Rega, 120, 121, 122, 123, 124,
    125, 126
Kaffir War (Cape War), 66
Kamrasi, 89, 91, 92, 93, 96, 120
Kandy, 9, 24, 26
Karka, 116
Khartoum, 4, 71, 77, 78, 79, 81, 82, 83,
    86, 87, 88, 89, 91, 97, 99, 100, 111,
    117, 124, 129, 132, 144, 154, 156,
    157, 158
Katchiba, 92
Kilimanjaro, 67
Kimberley, 99
Kinyon, 118
Kipling, Rudyard, 2, 5, 10, 16, 35
Kisuna, 126
Kitchener, Capt. Herbert, 10, 158
Kittakara, 122, 123
Korosoko, 72
Kossuth, Louis, 26, 54, 59
Kurshid, Aga, 86, 87, 91
Kutchuck Ali, 112, 113

Lahore, Treaty of, 50
Lejean, Guillaume, 83, 104
Leopold, King of the Belgians, 154
Liddell, Charles, 60
Little Big Horn, 131, 149
'Little Bob', 150
Livingstone, David, 66, 67, 71, 98, 99,
    105, 109, 112, 127, 129, 162
Login, Lady, 50, 52, 53, 58, 138
Login, Lord, 50
Lokko, 118
London, 11, 27
Luta N'zige, 89–94, 95, 97, 110, 112,
    116, 142

Luxor, 72
Lypiatt Park, 27

M'tesa, King of Uganda, 120, 127
MacCarra, Sandy, 46
Madras, 2, 146
Mahomet (dragoman), 72, 75, 78, 119
Malacca, 4
Marlborough Club, 143
Marshall, Rev. Robert, 105
Martin, Charlotte, 21, 46, 47
Martin, Rev. Charles, 21
Masindi, 120, 121, 123
Matonsé, 122
Mauritius, 13, 19, 21, 22–4
Maximilian, Emperor of Mexico, 118
McQueen, James, 100
McWilliam (engineer), 130, 133
Mecca, 68, 71
Mehemet Ali, 81
Mek Nimmur (Leopard King), 78, 83,
    105
Melville, Capt. Robert (Duleep Singh),
    52, 53
Metternich, Prince, 26, 53
Millais, John, 103
Milner, Lord, 6
Mohamed Wat-el-Mek, 119, 126, 127
Mohammed Ahmed (the Mahdi), 152,
    154, 158, 159, 162
Mohammed Ali, Khedive of Egypt, 4
Mohammed Deii, Captain, 117
Molyneux, Col. Charles, 134
Monsoor, Cpl., 117, 122, 123–4
Montgomerie, Captain, 101
Morlang, Franz, 86, 88
Morris, Col. William, 146
Mouche, Florian, 75, 77
Mozambique, 66–7
Murchison, Roderick, 66, 71, 97, 100,
    101, 103, 105, 131
Murie, Dr James, 82, 89, 91
Murray, Henry, 70, 71

Musa Pasha Hamdi, 83, 85
Mutesa, king of Buranda, 88, 89, 94

Napier, General Charles, 2, 21, 68
Napier, General Robert, 105–106
Napoleon III, Emperor of France, 107
Nassau, Maurice of, 22
New Zealand, 3, 4, 20
Newera Ellia, 9, 26–43, 45, 46, 146, 153
Nightingale, Florence, 19, 49
Nile Tributaries of Abyssinia, 104
Nolan, Capt. Louis, 133
North America, 3, 12, 13, 15
Nubar Pasha, 132

Oakley, Rev. John, 102
Omdurman, battle of, 10, 116
Osborne House, Isle of Wight, 50
Osman Digna, 152, 155, 156
Osprey, 153
Oswell, William, 71, 75, 103
Ottoman Empire, 4, 55, 57, 59, 107
Outram, James, 68
Oxford University, 5, 18, 67, 100

Paget (cutler), 34
Palliser, Edward, 38
Palmerston, Lord, 88, 102, 152
Paniadoli, 127
Paris, 26, 101, 107, 108, 129
Peel, Robert, 33–4
Perkes, Henry, 28, 29–30, 31
Petherick, John, 71, 73, 79, 81, 82, 83,
     86, 87, 88–9, 91, 98, 99, 100
Petherick, Katharine, 82, 88–9
Petőfi, Sandor, 51
Piccadilly, London, 34
Pimm, James, 20
Pitt, William the Elder (Earl of
     Chatham), 23
Pitt, William the Younger, 23

Poenaru, Petrache, 60
Port Louis, 25
Port Said, 21, 146
Portsmouth, 13
Powell, Maj., 149
Prester John, 65
Price, William, MP, 51, 60
Probyn, Lt., 157

Quat Kare, 113–4

Rahouka, 122
Ramadan (clerk), 121, 124
Ranjit Singh, 49
Raouf Bey, 114, 115, 116, 153
Regiments
   8th Hussars, 47–8, 101
   10th Hussars, 66, 79, 105, 133–4, 136,
      137, 156–7
   12th Lancers, 47–8, 63, 66
   19th Hussars, 158
   15th Foot, 25
   24th Foot, 122
   78th Highlanders, 88
   18th Bombay Infantry, 67
   46th Native Bengal Infantry, 67
   Ceylon Rifles, 31
   Royal Horse Guards, 155
   The Forty, 111–28, 141, 153
   Turkish Contingent, 48
Rhodes, Cecil, 99
Richarn, 85
Ridgeway Oaks, 14, 16
Rifle and Hound in Ceylon, 45
Rigby, Christopher, 73, 103
Rionga, 120, 126, 127
Rivers
   Atbara, 73
   Danube, 132
   Elbe, 53
   Nile, 4, 65–94, 95, 98, 100, 108, 110,
      111–28, 130, 131, 132, 133, 153,
      157, 158, 164

Spree, 53
Sutlej, 50
Zambezi, 66, 71, 98, 162
Roebuck, John, MP, 48
Rome, 27, 52, 58
Rorke's Drift, 122
Rot Jarma, 119
Rottingdean, 16, 17
Royal Geographical Society, 66, 68, 69, 70, 71, 73, 78, 84, 88, 95–101, 103, 130
Royal Humane Society, 113
Rugby, 49
Rugby School, 17
Ruskin, John, 5
Russell, Lord John, 72, 99
Russell, William, 106
Russian Empire, 4, 15
Russo-Turkish War, 144
Ruwenzori Mountains (Mountains of the Moon), 94

Saat, 85, 89
Saat (II), 118, 123
Sabanja, 49
Said, Wali of Egypt, 107
Sandford Orleigh, 133, 134, 141, 148, 154, 160, 164
Sandhurst, 48
Sapanga, 64
'Sarah', 75, 76
Sazasz, Madteos, 59
Schmidt, Johann, 76, 78, 84, 85, 97
Schweppes Company, 20
Scinde, 21, 68
Scutari, 49, 63
Sea of Marmara, 49, 63
Seacole, Mary, 48
Sebastopol, 48
Seeley, John, 8
Semlin, 53–4
Seroor, 127
Seymour, Admiral, 151–2
Shavolov, General, 139

Shaw, George Bernard, 7
Shaw, James, 132
Sheriff, Roder, 7
Sikhs, 49, 50
Slade, Major, 157
Smith O'Brien, William, 27
Smithfield, 11
Sofi, 74, 75, 76
Somerset, Fitzroy, Lord Raglan, 48
Speke, John, 56, 67–70, 78, 82, 84, 86, 87–9, 91, 93, 95, 96, 98, 99, 100, 101, 130, 162
Sri Lanka – see Ceylon
St James's Church, Piccadilly, 102
Stanley, Henry, 105, 127, 159
Stanley, Lord, 104
Stephenson, General, 156, 157
Stocks, Asst. Surgeon J.E., 68
Stoker, Bram, 101
Stradbroke, Countess of, 160
Strogan, Lt. William, 68
Stuart-Wortley, Lord Wharncliffe, 60, 66, 105, 110, 128, 136, 139, 147, 148
Suakin, 111, 152, 155, 156
Sudan, 4, 10, 58, 71, 74, 79, 82, 85, 107–28, 151–9, 162, 164
Suez Canal, 21, 69, 98, 107, 142, 144, 151
Suleiman, 120, 127
Sutherland, Duke of, 106, 138, 143

Tabora, 69
Taiping Rebellion, 131
Tanganyika, Lake, 69
Tapell, Mrs (governess), 47
Taramaki Wars, 3
Taskhessan, battle of, 143
Tasmania (Van Diemen's Land), 3
Tayib Agha, 114
Taylor, Bayard, 67
Tel-el-Kebir, battle of, 152
Tewfik, 113, 151, 152
Tewfikyeh (Sobat), 113, 114
'Texas Bill', 149

Thebes, 72
Theodore, Emperor of Abyssinia, 105
Thesiger, Frederick, Lord Chelmsford, 8
Thibault, Georges, 82, 83–4
Thistlewood, Arthur, 14
Thorngrove, 45
Thurston, Reverend, 9
Tinné, Alexandrine, 83, 84
Tinné, Harriet, 83, 84
Tipu Sahib, 2
Tokar, battle of, 155
Tottenham, 18, 19
Tottenham, Col. William, 49
Twain, Mark, 22

Uganda, 120, 161
United States of America – *see* North America
Unyoro, 119, 121, 123, 124, 126

Vacovia, 95
Valentia, Lord, 136
Vambery, Arminus, 101
van Capellan, Adriana, 83
Victoria, 3, 5, 18, 50, 53, 79, 91, 101, 108, 138, 146, 153
Victoria, Lake, 69, 70, 87, 89, 95, 110, 162

Vidin, 54, 56, 58, 59
Vienna, 26, 52, 53

Waikato Wars, 3
Wallfish Bay, 66
Ward, Roland, 159
Warren, Col., 144
Waterford, Marquess of, 138
Waterloo, Battle of, 13
Wellesley, Arthur, Duke of Wellington, 2, 17, 19, 27, 33
Whitehall Yard, 14, 16
Wilberforce, Bishop Samuel, 70, 100
Wilberforce, William, 14, 108, 129–30
Wild Beasts and Their Ways, 36, 39, 46, 160
Wilson, Charles, 158
Windham Club, 102
Wingate, Capt. Ronald, 139
Winterhalter, Franz, 50
Woking, 135, 163
Wolseley, Garnet, 145, 152, 157, 158
Wormald, Fanny, 156

Young England Movement, 28

Zanzibar, 69, 73, 103, 131
Zobieir Pasha, 155